Essential Business Skills for Social Work Managers

Many social workers find themselves in management positions within a few years of graduating from MSW programs. Most of these jobs are in nonprofit human service organizations in which, increasingly, business acumen is necessary to maintain grants and donations, start new programs, market services to clients, supervise the finance function, and understand the external environment.

This book teaches MSW students and early-stage social work management practitioners the essential business skills needed to manage programs and organizations; to improve their overall management toolkit for finding a better job or getting promoted; and, ultimately, to gain parity with other managers holding MBA degrees and working in the human service space.

This text can serve as a desk reference for managers to troubleshoot various situations. It is also appropriate for social work macro practice courses at the undergraduate and graduate levels, as well as courses that cover human resource management and financial management.

Andrew J. Germak, MBA, MSW, is executive director of the Center for Leadership and Management and professor of professional practice at the School of Social Work at Rutgers, the State University of New Jersey. His prior appointment at Rutgers was executive director of the Institute for Families, where he served for over three years. Previously, Germak served as president and CEO of the Mental Health Association of Morris County, Inc., and also held a variety of leadership and direct service positions in the nonprofit human service sector. He has authored editorial columns and letters appearing in leading publications, such as the *Wall Street Journal* and *Financial Times*. His 2010 academic article, "Social Entrepreneurship: Changing the Way Social Workers Do Business," has been widely influential. Germak received his MBA from NYU Stern School of Business, his MSW from the Silberman School of Social Work at Hunter College in New York, and his BA in Psychology from the University of Michigan at Ann Arbor.

Essential Business Skills for Social Work Managers

Tools for Optimizing Programs and Organizations

Andrew J. Germak

NEW YORK AND LONDON

First published 2015
by Routledge
711 Third Avenue, New York, NY 10017

and by Routledge
2 Park Square, Milton Park, Abingdon, Oxon, OX14 4RN

Routledge is an imprint of the Taylor & Francis Group, an informa business

© 2015 Taylor & Francis

The right of Andrew J. Germak to be identified as author of this
work has been asserted by him in accordance with sections 77 and 78
of the Copyright, Designs and Patents Act 1988.

All rights reserved. No part of this book may be reprinted or reproduced
or utilized in any form or by any electronic, mechanical, or other means,
now known or hereafter invented, including photocopying and recording,
or in any information storage or retrieval system, without permission in
writing from the publishers.

Trademark notice: Product or corporate names may be trademarks or
registered trademarks, and are used only for identification and
explanation without intent to infringe.

Library of Congress Cataloging in Publication Data
Germak, Andrew J.
  Essential business skills for social work managers: tools for optimizing
  programs and organizations/by Andrew J. Germak.
  pages cm
  1. Social work administration. 2. Management. I. Title.
  HV40.G46 2015
  361.0068'4—dc23
  2014021750

ISBN: 978-0-415-64392-4 (hbk)
ISBN: 978-0-415-64393-1 (pbk)
ISBN: 978-1-315-77603-3 (ebk)

Typeset in Adobe Caslon and Copperplate
by Florence Production Ltd, Stoodleigh, Devon, UK

To all of my former and current co-workers,
students, teachers, and mentors
from whom I have learned and continue
to learn so much about this work.

CONTENTS

PREFACE   XIII

ACKNOWLEDGMENTS   XVII

1 THE CHANGING NATURE OF SOCIAL WORK MANAGEMENT   1

Practice Example: The Social Work Manager as Salesperson 2

The Social Work Manager's Environment: How Has It Evolved? 5

Social Entrepreneurship: Changing the Way Social Workers Do Business 7

Defining Social Entrepreneurship 8

Social Entrepreneurship: Current Practice 9

A Social Work Manager's Reactions to a Changing Environment 11

Where Do Businesslike Social Work Managers Work? 14

    Nonprofit Organizations *14*

    For-Profit Organizations *16*

    Hybrid Organizations *17*

    Other Types of Organizations *17*

VIII   CONTENTS

Essential Business Skills for Social Work Managers:
   Key Domains   18
Chapter Summary   19
Suggested Learning Exercises   20
Internet Resources   21

2   FINANCIAL MANAGEMENT   25

The Importance of Financial Health   26
Understanding the Financial Health of Your Program
   or Organization   28
Basics of Nonprofit Accounting   28
The Balance Sheet   32
The Income Statement   33
The Statement of Cash Flows   36
Projecting Revenue and Expense   38
Annualizing Revenue and Expense   39
Building Pro Forma Financial Statements   41
Understanding Nonprofit Capital Structure   43
Chapter Summary   45
Suggested Learning Exercises   46
Internet Resources   46

3   TALENT MANAGEMENT   49

Practice Example: Balancing Financial and Talent
   Management   50
Social Work as a Service Business   52
   The Relationship between Customer and Service Provider   53
   Using Feedback from Customers in Decision-Making   54
Managing Downward   55
   Developing the Talent Pipeline   56
   Making Optimal Hiring Decisions   57
   Structuring the Workforce   58
   Performance Management and Talent Development   61
   Taking Care of Your People: The Total Compensation View   62
Managing Upward   63
   Board Relations and Board Development   64

CONTENTS IX

Succession Planning 65
Supervisor Relations 65
Adding Value through Stretch Assignments 66
Perspectives from the Field: Working with a Board of Directors 67
Managing Sideways 71
Developing Strategic Networks 72
Internal versus External Connections 72
Social Networking as a Talent Management Tool 73
Chapter Summary 73
Suggested Learning Exercises 74
Internet Resources 75

4 MARKETING, SALES, AND COMMUNICATIONS 79

Marketing Is More Than Just Advertising 80
Common Marketing Frameworks: Four P's and STP 80
Conducting Market Research 85
Developing a Marketing Plan 85
Selling Internally 87
Getting Everyone on Board with Your Mission and
Ideas 88
Motivating Your Team to Develop and Execute New
Business 88
Promoting Ideas to Current Customers, Organization Staff,
and Others 89
Selling Externally 89
Prospective Customers 90
The Board of Directors 91
Funders 91
Media 91
Other Stakeholders 92
Communications Essentials 92
The 30-Second Elevator Pitch 93
The Two-Minute Pitch 94
Conducting Meetings in a Businesslike Manner 95
E-Mail Etiquette 95
Recognizing and Thanking Everyone 97

CONTENTS

Chapter Summary 98
Suggested Learning Exercises 99
Internet Resources 100

5 THE BUSINESS PLAN 103

The Rationale for Business Planning 104
Basic Components of a Business Plan 107
    Executive Summary 108
    Program Concept 109
    Market and Competition Analysis 109
    Marketing Plan 111
    Operations Plan 112
    Financial Plan 112
    Management Team Information 113
    Appendices 114
Perspectives from the Field: Business Planning in a Social
   Work Setting 116
Chapter Summary 116
Suggested Learning Exercises 117
Internet Resources 118

6 IMPACT, SUSTAINABILITY, AND EFFECTIVENESS/ PERFORMANCE MEASUREMENT 121

Defining Impact, Sustainability, and Effectiveness/Performance 123
Measuring Program or Organizational Effectiveness/Performance 125
    Outputs versus Outcomes 126
    How For-Profit Organizations Measure Effectiveness/
    Performance 129
    Is Effectiveness/Performance Measurement of Social
    Work Programs and Organizations Possible? 130
Using Logic Models to Guide the Measurement Process 132
Perspectives from the Field: Impact, Sustainability, and
   Measurement 133
Chapter Summary 136
Suggested Learning Exercises 137
Internet Resources 137

CONTENTS

7 EMERGING ISSUES IN POLICY, ETHICS, AND NEW TECHNOLOGY   139

    An Unfavorable Business Climate Is Developing 140
    Ethical Considerations for Social Entrepreneurship and
        Businesslike Social Work Management 143
    New Technology and the Human Services 146
        E-Mail 147
        Social Media 148
        Mobile Devices and Apps 150
    Chapter Summary 151
    Suggested Learning Exercises 152
    Internet Resources 153

8 CONCLUSION   155

    Review of Key Points from All Chapters 155
    Closing Remarks 160

APPENDIX 1: PARENT UNIVERSE—PROFILE OF A SOCIAL ENTERPRISE FOUNDED BY A SOCIAL WORKER   161

APPENDIX 2: PARENT UNIVERSE—DISCUSSION QUESTIONS   165

APPENDIX 3: PARENT UNIVERSE—A PLACE FOR PARENTS WHO THINK THE WORLD OF THEIR CHILDREN: BUSINESS PLAN   167

GLOSSARY OF KEY TERMS AND CONCEPTS   207

REFERENCES   215

INDEX   221

PREFACE

Yes, I have written a book that combines the fields of business and social work—two subjects that do not often go together, I realize. Admittedly, some in our field may have an adverse reaction to my embrace of business practices. Still, my experience tells me that the trend is unavoidable despite what may be ideological objections from some in the social work field. Having pursued my Master of Social Work (MSW) and Master of Business Administration (MBA) in recent years and managed various social work programs and projects in the process, it continues to concern me how few business management concepts—most often taught in MBA programs—are explored in social work educational programs and utilized by social workers in the management and leadership ranks of human service organizations.

Social work managers often wonder why "those MBAs" are taking over the leadership of human service programs and organizations. I believe social workers are losing leadership ground to other professionals because we are not learning enough about the business side of our work, which has become a necessary aspect of successful social work management.

It is widely known that many social workers find themselves in supervisory and management positions within a few years of graduating from MSW programs. Many of these jobs are in nonprofit human service organizations in which, increasingly, business acumen is necessary to maintain grants and donations, start new programs, market services to clients, supervise the finance function, understand the external environment, and so forth. Even within public-sector settings, many of these business skills are still relevant and necessary. Yet, our training generally does not place enough emphasis on the depth of management acumen a social worker needs to succeed as an organizational manager and leader.

Therefore, I present you with this introductory book describing these necessary business management skills in one place. I have written this book for students and social work managers from my perspective as a fellow social work manager. There is a saying in management, "It's lonely at the top," which describes the feelings of isolation that managers and leaders experience as they advance within organizations. I have felt this way plenty of times in my career. My hope is that this book can help minimize some of the loneliness that you may feel as you rise in your career.

My students and colleagues often ask me why I decided to pursue an MBA after my MSW. I usually tell them that I wanted to run a nonprofit organization and needed to obtain more business management skills than were taught to me during my MSW program in order to land the job I wanted. Each day in my role as a nonprofit manager and executive (and still today in my administrative academic position), I have drawn on the knowledge base of my MBA training, as well as the social work foundation of my MSW. I find this combination to be optimal for managing a human service operation.

Additionally, students in MSW classes that I teach have asked me if getting an MBA is required to move up the ladder in social work management (they know that I have one and want to know my "inside opinion"). The MBA is an arduous albeit rewarding path to take, but admittedly it is not for everyone. I truly believe that this book could help you forego, or at least delay, the MBA. Getting an advanced business degree may not be as necessary as some might think to reach the top of a human service organization, and believe me when I tell you that it is quite expensive to pursue this path!

In summary, this book should help social work undergraduate and MSW students, and early-stage social work management practitioners:

(1) understand the essential business skills needed to manage programs and organizations; (2) improve their overall management toolkit for finding a better job or getting promoted; (3) serve as a desk reference for managers to troubleshoot various real-world situations; and (4) ultimately, gain parity with other managers and leaders holding MBA or other management degrees and working in the human service space.

For teaching purposes, this book would be most appropriate for social work macro practice courses at the undergraduate and graduate levels. Specifically, this book could be used as a supplemental text for macro practice foundation courses. The first chapter, for example, could be a useful assigned reading to help students understand the changing nature of social work management. The appendix case profile and discussion questions could be used as a teaching tool (or an assigned class project) for the macro practice foundation course. Additionally, some schools of social work offer courses in human resource management, financial management, and so forth. The chapters in this book that deal with these specific topics could be assigned reading in these types of courses. The suggested learning exercises included at the end of each chapter could serve as class assignments.

To the students using this book in class and to others practicing social work management, I trust that you will find this book helpful as you navigate your career as a social work manager. If I can be of any assistance to you along the way, please do not hesitate to let me know. Keeping our professional network alive and strong is a key to our success in the field of social work management.

Andrew J. Germak
New Brunswick, New Jersey
May 21, 2014

ACKNOWLEDGMENTS

I could not have completed this book without the support of my loving wife, Victorina, and our two small children, John and Victorina. I have written many things in my life thus far, none of which have required the focus and concentration required to produce a book. The patience that my family has had with me throughout this process has been unwavering.

I am also indebted to my staff at the Center for Leadership and Management, the Institute for Families, my colleagues at Rutgers School of Social Work, and to the staff and board at the Mental Health Association of Morris County, Inc., my prior employer, for providing me with excellent executive-level experiences and supportive work environments. My early mentors at Fedcap in New York City also deserve recognition and thanks, especially the supervisor of my first management job, Maureen Bentley, and my MSW field instructor, Bryan Warde, both of whom dedicated much time to helping me develop as a manager and leader.

Finally, I thank Dick Edwards for believing in me enough to hire me as a faculty member at Rutgers School of Social Work and for his support of this book project. Likewise, I wish to thank Jim Blackburn, Leon Ginsberg, and Shelly Wimpfheimer for their helpful advice and support during this process. The reviewers of earlier versions of this book also deserve my appreciation; their comments were very helpful in refining this book for publication:

- Bryan Warde (Lehman College)
- Bill Waldman (Rutgers)
- Leon Ginsberg (Appalachian State University)
- Thom Reilly (San Diego State University)

Many thanks also to my editor, Steve Rutter, associate editor, Samantha Barbaro, and everyone at Routledge for their extreme patience as I produced this book, which ended up taking much longer to write than they had hoped. Lastly, to all of my friends and colleagues at the Network for Social Work Management, I thank you for your ongoing support of my career and the careers of so many social work managers throughout the nation and the world.

1

THE CHANGING NATURE OF SOCIAL WORK MANAGEMENT

This book is essentially about developing certain business skills that can be used to be most effective as a social work manager in a variety of organizational contexts. Indeed, business and social work are two disciplines that have not always shared common ground, although the two fields do have some overlapping attributes and recommended skill sets in common. If you are an undergraduate or graduate student in social work, you may not have yet had the opportunity to take courses in financial management, human resources, marketing, and so forth. As a practitioner managing social work programs and organizations, you may also need some additional help with the business management aspects of your work, especially if you did not learn about these related topics in your social work degree program. The time has come for social workers—especially those that manage human service programs and organizations—to develop a basic toolkit in business management practices. This book is designed to assist you in developing such a toolkit.

To set the stage for skill development in subsequent chapters, this introductory chapter will make the case that social work management in the human service sector has evolved in recent years. I will explain why it is important for the contemporary social work manager to develop business acumen and embrace a new form of management practice often referred to as social entrepreneurship—essentially, the blending of business management techniques with social work macro practice. I will provide a case example of what it feels like to be working as a social work manager in a businesslike or entrepreneurial agency environment. Further, I will discuss the types of organizations that employ social work managers and explain how being businesslike and entrepreneurial can help you add value to these organizations. A strong grasp of the content and especially the tone of this first chapter should help you to navigate the skill development chapters that follow.

Practice Example: The Social Work Manager as Salesperson

I remember sitting at my desk one early morning a few years back while I was serving as president and chief executive officer of a midsized nonprofit human service organization dedicated to advocacy and empowerment for people living with serious mental illness. It was just before 8:00 a.m. and I was attending to my usual routine of reading and responding to the flow of e-mails that had arrived overnight (no matter how late I stayed up working the night before, it seemed that there were always other dedicated colleagues of mine that worked even later into the night than I did and, consequently, it was not uncommon to receive a string of e-mails starting at 2:00 a.m. from various people in my professional network). Then, the phone rang. It was the president of the local chamber of commerce.

"Good morning, Andy, we're looking for a nonprofit CEO to address a large audience of corporate executives and local political leaders on Thursday at 7:00 a.m. This is part of a series of nonprofit CEO presentations designed to let our chamber members know about the services that nonprofits provide in our region. We've built these presentations into our monthly breakfast networking meetings," he said. "Lots of influential and potentially helpful people will be there—about 200 or so are expected—should be a great opportunity to showcase your agency. Are you interested?"

"You mean this Thursday . . . in two days? What type of presentation are you looking for?" I asked.

"Yes, the event is on Thursday and you'll have about 90 seconds at the beginning of the program to talk about your agency's mission and its services to the community. It's a tight program. No formal presentation needed—just a chance to get up and make a pitch about what you do. Sound good?"

"Yes, sounds great. I'll be there!" I replied emphatically, although I must admit that I was somewhat nervous. Ninety seconds was not a lot of time to talk about my *entire* organization!

Take a minute right now and try to describe your organization or program. Can you do it in 90 seconds? Can you even do it in less than two minutes? In less than five minutes? Don't worry. Most social work managers and leaders that I have heard speak about their programs and organizations—whether nonprofit, public sector, or for-profit—cannot do it easily. In fact, when I first started working as a social work manager, I was not able to succinctly describe the program I directed either. It takes practice!

Furthermore, on that phone call the president of the chamber of commerce made it clear to me in his request that a "formal presentation" was not necessary at the event. However, I cannot emphasize enough that there is no such thing as an informal presentation when one is a social work manager. Every appearance in public—both within your organization at staff meetings, board meetings, and so forth, and outside of your agency at events such as this chamber of commerce breakfast—should be viewed as a formal presentation that requires careful planning and preparation to be an effective one. Far too often, you only get one chance to make a strong impression.

Presentations: There is no such thing as an informal presentation. Every public appearance requires careful planning and preparation. You may only get one chance to make a strong impression.

Figure 1.1 Management Tip

Fortunately, I had had some preparation for giving this type of concise sales pitch and knew that, with a little practice, I would do just fine at the chamber of commerce event on Thursday morning. During business school, my classmates and I were asked as part of a career development program to develop two-minute pitches in which we were to describe our strengths and career aspirations in a very concise manner for prospective employers. Together, we literally practiced this exercise over and over with a timer until we were able to master it. It took a bit of time but we finally mastered the process and were prepared, at least in this regard, for forthcoming job interviews.

In addition to being ready for job interviews, this business school exercise also prepared me to effectively represent myself and my organization in public. Because of this training, what my colleague from the chamber of commerce was inviting me to do was not extremely foreign to me. I just needed to practice my sales pitch for the specific human service organization for which I worked as an executive (that was the first time I had done that in that particular job). So, the routine of my day changed at that point. I began to monitor the second hand on my watch and started talking out loud to myself in my office, practicing my pitch for Thursday.

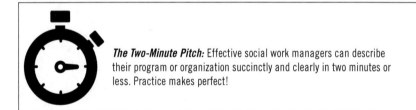

Figure 1.2 Key Skill

This practice example is one among many possible social work management situations for which I suggest that possessing business acumen—in this case, the requisite skills involved in communicating succinctly and making a sales pitch—can help social work managers excel in the human services industry. I will discuss marketing, sales, and communications in more detail in Chapter 4, but for now I would like to convey to you the need to develop a toolkit of business skills in order to maximize your effectiveness in a human service industry that has evolved into a highly competitive and often unforgiving marketplace. In the example above, I was one of many nonprofit CEOs that had been asked to make an appearance at an event in my local area. This event was representative of events occurring across the country on any given day in which human service leaders are asked to make public appearances, often with the underlying objective of attracting new support for the leaders' organizations. Hence, competition for funding, strong volunteers, board members, and so forth was definitely part of my daily life as president and chief executive officer—and plays a large role in any social work manager's job.

Being comfortable with sales pitches, for instance, has helped me to raise funds, develop new social work programs, and build strategic organizational partnerships and alliances. Other important business skills (financial management, talent management, marketing, communications, and so forth), some of which were briefly introduced to me during my MSW program and I later refined in business school, have also helped me perform successfully as a social work manager. All of these skills will be discussed in this book. But first, here is some background on how social work management has recently evolved to become a more businesslike practice, which should help to frame this book's content—and the reasons for which I decided to write it.

The Social Work Manager's Environment: How Has It Evolved?

My social work management colleagues that are much more experienced than I am frequently tell me that management in the human service sector has changed substantially over the past few decades and, I would argue, even more rapidly over the past 10 years since I started working as a manager in this field. Specifically, today's social work managers face the following common challenges in the oversight of human service organizations (Wimpfheimer & Germak, 2012):

- Strong focus on program *outcomes* as opposed to simply *outputs*
- Demands for *transparency* and *accountability*
- Emphasis on *risk management* in a *constrained resource environment*
- Expectations for *evidence-based practice*
- *Reduced resources* from traditional funding sources
- The *need for diversification* of funding streams

- Substantial *competition* from nonprofits and for-profits
- Ongoing *oversight, vigilance,* and *regulation* from *diverse stakeholders*

If any of the above issues resonate with you (or if you do not know what some of them mean), then keep reading. This book should help you to mitigate these management challenges to some degree and sustain your needed social work programs and organizations into the future.

The operating environment for social work organizations of all types, especially in the United States, has evolved since many of them were founded decades ago and has presented significant challenges to the traditional model in which such organizations are managed (Germak and Singh, 2010). A notable and very recent example of this phenomenon is the closure of Hull House in Chicago, the iconic settlement house founded by social work pioneer Jane Addams in 1889. The organization recently closed its doors ostensibly due to some of the common

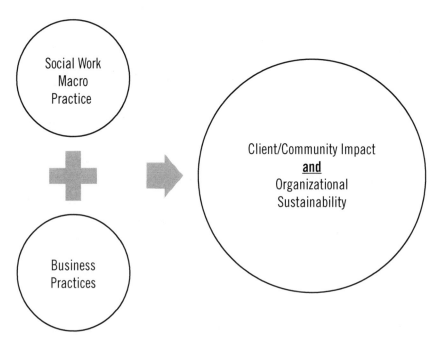

Figure 1.3 Contemporary Social Work Management
Source: Wimpfheimer and Germak (2012)

pressures related to contemporary social work management mentioned above: ill-preparedness for a highly competitive environment, non-diversified funding streams, reduced resources from traditional sources, and other similar challenges (Cohen, 2012).

To survive these current management challenges, even within longstanding and seemingly stable human service organizations, I argue that the job orientation and associated skills of the social work managers and leaders of such organizations need to evolve to become more businesslike and entrepreneurial. Social work management practice today requires that social workers leading programs and organizations adopt a business management orientation that, first and foremost, includes a focus on social impact (a focus on outcomes more than simply program outputs), as well as financial sustainability (more than an ongoing dependence on traditional sources of funding), as depicted in Figure 1.3 and as explained henceforth. Moreover, Chapter 6 includes a lengthier discussion of the concepts of impact and sustainability, and how they can be appropriately measured in human service organizations.

Social Entrepreneurship: Changing the Way Social Workers Do Business[1]

In November each year, the *New York Times* publishes a special section of the newspaper (also available at: www.nytimes.com/pages/giving/) entitled "Giving," which discusses recent trends in philanthropy and highlights cutting-edge social programs that have emerged around the world. The cover stories in recent years have profiled various individuals and businesslike organizations—Jeffrey Skoll, Stephen Case, Pierre Omidyar, Richard Branson, Bono, Ted Turner, The Acumen Fund, and Google—dedicated to ridding the world of its multitude of social problems. In the sections' lead articles and the subsequent dozens of pages of reports regarding groundbreaking social service work, there are almost never any references to social workers and their contributions. Undoubtedly, social work professionals are some of the individuals best prepared to respond to the world's social problems. Despite our training, however, in the current realm of forward-looking, functional solutions to complex societal challenges, social workers are not easy to find in the solution mix of societal problem solving.

Given the tremendous need for creative solutions to today's complex social problems, social workers should embrace the straightforward business sense found in a practice called *social entrepreneurship*, essentially a hybrid phenomenon of social work macro practice principles and business innovation activities. Many social workers are already exposed to a businesslike sector by virtue of their working in nonprofit organization environments. Encompassing nearly 1.6 million organizations and representing some 5.5 percent of the gross domestic product of the United States (Independent Sector, 2013), the nonprofit sector in the United States, for example, is a robust socioeconomic influence. Not only is the American nonprofit industry sizeable and growing, but also it exists in an increasingly competitive marketplace in which nonprofit administrators routinely vie for limited funds (Lewis, Packard, & Lewis, 2012; Salamon, 1999).

Social workers and the human service agencies that they manage sit squarely in the midst of this competition. As responsible social work management professionals, we would be remiss not to *mind our own business* and join the ever-increasing ranks of the "social entrepreneurs." Indeed, embracing the practice of social entrepreneurship involves changing the way social workers do business, but being businesslike has become such a necessary attribute of successfully managing contemporary social work programs and organizations—it is time to change our mindset.

Defining Social Entrepreneurship

According to Mosher-Williams (2006), there is no commonly accepted definition of what social entrepreneurship is and how it may be distinguished from companion terms such as social enterprise, nonprofit entrepreneurship, social venturing, social purpose business development, venture philanthropy, and so on. First, social entrepreneurship is broadly defined as the programmatic and fiscal innovation associated with realizing social change (Harding, 2004; Roberts & Woods, 2005). Dart (2004) supposes that nonprofit agencies, for instance, that embrace social entrepreneurship operate in a much more businesslike fashion than do straightforward and traditional nonprofits. Likewise, Brewster (2006) illustrates that social entrepreneurship looks vastly different from traditional fundraising and development. Moreover, it may be conceptualized differently in various contexts and regions of the world, which adds to its conceptual complexity (Kerlin, 2010).

Despite the different conceptualizations, the core concept is always identical: social entrepreneurship comprises innovative ideas for social change executed utilizing sound business strategies and skills. Paul Light's (2006) working definition of a social entrepreneur is a good framework for this discussion. Light describes a social entrepreneur as "an individual, group, network, organization, or alliance of organizations that seeks sustainable, large-scale change through pattern breaking ideas in what or how governments, nonprofits, and businesses do to address significant social problems" (p. 50). Essentially, social entrepreneurship, as it relates to the focus of this book, is a broad umbrella-like concept that includes not only businesslike and entrepreneurial start-up activities undertaken to launch new social work organizations and programs, but also innovative management practices executed within more mature organizations, such as Hull House, and even within certain public sector (i.e. government) organizations that allow for innovation and enterprising behavior.

Social Entrepreneurship: innovative ideas for social change executed utilizing sound business management strategies and skills.

Figure 1.4 Key Concept

Social Entrepreneurship: Current Practice

Due to the decreased availability of government grants and the earmarked nature of charitable donations, entrepreneurial social work managers typically begin their work by developing nontraditional avenues for generating sufficient revenue to run social programs so that they can ultimately provide quality services for clients. According to Froelich (1999) and Anderson, Dees, and Emerson (2002), such revenue diversification strategies in a nonprofit organization, for instance, might include development of mission-related businesses, commercial activity unrelated to an agency's mission, mergers with other nonprofits, partnerships with venture philanthropists, and so forth. In fact, Weisbrod (1998) posits that of all revenue streams available to nonprofit organizations, revenue from commercial activity is the most useful to an agency's mission due to its unrestricted nature, and therefore such income streams should become more utilized by nonprofits seeking to sustain their services.

Further, it is argued that as commercial activity increases in a nonprofit human service organization, the more its leadership must embrace common business principles (Firstenberg, 1986). The most common business principle understood by social entrepreneurs involves the classic economic theory of supply and demand. Simply stated, price is in equilibrium (optimal) when the quantity of a product or service offered equals the price someone is willing to pay for the product or service (Samuelson & Marks, 2003). In social work settings, this theory can be applied by first determining the total capacity of a service, then examining the client utilization rate. The higher the utilization rate, the closer a service is to being in equilibrium. However, according to Brinckerhoff (2000), practitioners too often create programs based on what they think clients need instead of services in which they are willing to partake. Thus, programs endure for years at times (the *supply* part of the theory) without regard for the actual *demand*. How often do social work managers perform market research to determine whether a true market demand exists for the services they provide (more on market research in Chapter 4)? On the contrary, Bornstein (2004) argues that successful social entrepreneurs listen closely to what people want and respond with optimal programs that address their specific demands.

One well-known example of an entrepreneurial social program developed to address a market demand is Grameen Bank. The joint winners of the 2006 Nobel Peace Prize, Muhammad Yunus (founder of the organization) and Grameen Bank, have successfully addressed the demand for economic independence in Bangladesh by establishing a vast system of microcredit. Since 1976, Yunus's Grameen Bank has made micro-loans—as little as $30 each—to economically disadvantaged Bangladeshis, many of whom are women, and, consequently, helped 5.3 million people build credit, support their families, construct homes, start small businesses, and move toward economic independence. Historically, since few micro-loans have defaulted and there exists an ever-increasing demand for such loans, Yunus has been able to develop his bank to a point at which it both makes a profit and serves the poor— a truly impactful and sustainable social enterprise (Norwegian Nobel Committee, 2006). In addition, the success of Grameen Bank's business model has led to the development of 48 other related social enterprise-type firms, from textiles to telecommunications, in the Grameen family of companies (*The Economist*, 2012).

From this short profile of the work of Muhammad Yunus, one should realize that social entrepreneurship or general businesslike activity, when successful, can alleviate certain social problems and potentially spawn other much needed enterprises. Essentially, the fiscal stability of a social enterprise-type organization and the availability of profits allow for business growth, which is not frequently seen in traditional social work organizations. For instance, how many social work managers ask themselves, "If only we had funding for that service?" Social work managers who embrace social entrepreneurship can stop asking that question and begin realizing the services they desire.

Now let us turn to a brief profile of a social work manager who works for a businesslike nonprofit human service organization and who is embracing this new way of doing business. For further study, there is also a profile and a sample business plan of an actual social enterprise included as an appendix to this book, but I recommend that you continue reading at least through Chapter 5 in order to learn some basic concepts before trying to learn from this in-depth case example.

A Social Work Manager's Reactions to a Changing Environment

I recently had the opportunity to meet with a social work manager, Samantha, who works for a community-based nonprofit human service organization in my local area and talk with her about her work, especially how she approaches her social work practice with a businesslike perspective.[2] Given her businesslike mindset, I would classify this social worker as a social entrepreneur, even though she works for a larger and more traditional nonprofit organization and does not necessarily think of herself as an entrepreneur. It is true that social workers are largely absent from the public discourse on social entrepreneurship as described above, yet they do exist within various organizations if one looks hard enough and unpacks the business nature of their work.

Indeed, a few strong themes emerged from my conversation with Samantha. First, she viewed being businesslike in her work—in this case, operating a social work program with a fee-for-service revenue model—as one of the only options for raising funds in the current resource-constrained economic climate. In response to a question I asked about her approach to general fundraising for social service programs, she replied:

> Our agency has been, really the last couple of years looking for different ways to bring new funding into our agency as opposed to the traditional grant writing approach to try to find monies. It has been very difficult in the last few years with a lot of cuts federally and state-wise to continue to fund our programs and whenever we do get funding it is really for a very restricted targeted populations and we feel that our reach isn't extensive enough with the kind of monies we can get strictly from grant resources. So we have been talking actually for a few years . . . figuring out ways we can bring fee-for-service type programming into the agency and . . . and look at other ways of funding as opposed to the traditional approach.

I asked how this new approach has been going for her and for the organization. She responded, "Our biggest struggle is, like how we are, how much we could actually charge for a visit? What would the market be able to sustain?" I asked her why she thought that she and her colleagues were struggling with this particular pricing issue. Samantha replied:

> I guess you know traditionally [social workers] weren't even paid people, we were volunteers you know going out to help others and that . . . if you do that and accept money for it . . . that's you know . . . you aren't supposed to do that, you are supposed

CHANGES IN SOCIAL WORK MANAGEMENT 13

to be volunteering and it is all for goodwill kind of thing and so I think because of our roots we are never considered paid employees of agencies doing this kind of work that it probably has just continued that way over the years where you know if you did have to charge for anything it had to be subsidized or sliding scale or you know you always tried to figure out ways to get the services for the lowest cost possible. And you never think, you know, how are we going to make money from something? So it has always been hard for me to ask for money in exchange for services anyway. I always end up under billing if I ever did anything anyway so . . . it is hard. That is just the philosophy that we grew up with.

I asked Samantha whether she felt, as I do, that social workers should embrace a business mindset, albeit with some additional training in order to sustain essential client services into the future. She responded in the following way, which is consistent with the discussion of social workers embracing social entrepreneurship that I introduced in the previous sections of this chapter:

We need to be growing as a profession and we need to be looking at different ways to collaborate and if it is going to bring in business, great. You know, we are good at building partnerships so I think it is a natural, you know, that we are looking at partnering in the business world, in the business community and, you know, getting resources differently and learning that it is OK to do that. So I think it is about time and I . . . you know . . . we need it to be able to grow as a profession.

The quotations from Samantha included here are meant to give you a real-world view of how social entrepreneurship or, more generally speaking, businesslike social work management manifests itself among contemporary social work managers working in social work and human service organizations. As you can see from Samantha's experience at her nonprofit human service organization, the path toward social entrepreneurship or businesslike social work management in reality is not an easy one for social workers. There is often resistance to changing the way we deliver social services. Furthermore, there is frequent unease with discussions of money and financial management. You may be feeling some of these things in your field placement or in the organization where you work. During the MSW program, we are not often taught how to properly price our program's services, for example. There are many other business activities for which social workers are not sufficiently trained. My hope is that you, as a social work student and emerging leader, will begin to raise these types of issues in class, in fieldwork, and in practice in order to develop your skills in this area *before* you begin working as middle managers, executives, and key decision-makers in the human services. Earning enough revenue as an organization to sustain social programs, for instance, is a modern reality regardless of the type of organization for which you work. Going into a management job with some familiarity and comfort with this particular issue will be extremely valuable.

Where Do Businesslike Social Work Managers Work?

You may be wondering where, as you read this book and continue to hone your skills as a social work manager, you could find a meaningful job as a businesslike or entrepreneurial social work manager—as a social entrepreneur. Despite this chapter's focus on innovative and entrepreneurial organizations, business-oriented social work managers are needed by and employed by a variety of types of organizations, not just entrepreneurial, start-up-type organizations. For the most part, social work managers are employed by the following types of organizations, as represented in Table 1.1 and described below: nonprofit, for-profit, hybrid, and other types of organizations.

Nonprofit Organizations

Nonprofit organizations are where the majority of social workers end up spending their careers. Essentially, nonprofits are private corporations that are dedicated to the public good. Nonprofit organizations are independent from government or other auspices in a legal sense, and have no owners or shareholders (Hopkins, 2009). Many of the larger human service nonprofit organizations can feel quite corporate, whereas

Table 1.1 Organizations Employing Businesslike Social Work Managers

Organization Type	Examples	How Social Work Managers Add Value
Nonprofit	• community behavioral health • child and family services • advocacy and grassroots organizations	• maximize efficiency and effectiveness of existing programs • launch social enterprise projects as nonprofit subsidiaries • manage for growth
For-profit	• mental and physical healthcare • managed care • residential programs • specialized addiction clinics • prison healthcare	• leverage resources of company and grow and expand services • use social work values to enhance organizational culture • maintain emphasis on social objectives even when profit is paramount
Hybrid	• social enterprises • job training programs • micro-lending institutions	• balance profit-making goals with client-oriented outcomes • understand client point of view and incorporate into planning and operations
Other	• government entities • economic development authorities • policy think tanks • universities	• develop macro-level policies • maintain focus on clients amid demanding stakeholder environment • impart management knowledge through teaching, training, research, and publication

smaller, grassroots organizations may be more volunteer driven and less professionalized. Nonetheless, within any of these organizations are ample opportunities for entrepreneurial and businesslike social work managers to make a difference. A good example of this is Samantha's organization to which I alluded in the previous section. This is a traditional nonprofit that is veering into more entrepreneurial projects in order to diversify its revenue streams and sustain its programs. Whether it be supervising a program and maximizing its efficiency and effectiveness by employing your business skills, or managing a social venture that is a for-profit subsidiary of a larger nonprofit organization, business skills are sought after in nonprofit organizations. The main benefit of working in a nonprofit is that the primary focus of the organization is its social mission, which translates into the organization keeping an emphasis on helping its service beneficiaries and clients as the primary objective of the organization.

For-Profit Organizations

For-profit companies may look similar to nonprofits, especially to large nonprofits, but there is a fundamental difference. For-profits are primarily focused on making money for owners or shareholders. For-profit organizations may be private or public, but the distinguishing feature, regardless of type of ownership, is that for-profits are owned by individuals or groups of individuals, and proceeds earned from the business may flow to the owners. For example, many social services, such as psychiatric and medical care services, have been privatized in prison systems throughout the United States. What this means is that for-profit firms are managing these social services for the prison population instead of the government (or a nonprofit organization) managing them. Indeed, some of these companies are public and listed on major stock exchanges. This allows them to sell ownership shares (i.e. stock) to the public. When a company is organized as a for-profit, especially when it is a publicly traded firm, the focus first and foremost is on maximizing profit for shareholders, who are the owners of the company. These types of companies, therefore, may cut some corners in order to meet profit targets and maximize the return to shareholders. Frequently, profits are made without a focus on quality of care in social work settings. Still, for-profit companies do hire social workers and these environments can be good places of employment for the business-minded social work manager, as often there are more resources at one's disposal, the organizations tend to be more nimble, and the compensation packages can be quite comprehensive. Moreover, there is opportunity for a social work manager to make a real difference within such organizations. On the other hand, as opposed to nonprofits, a social work manager in a for-profit environment should know that the primary focus of the for-profit organization may not be client well-being to the extent that well-being does not translate into increased profits for the company.

Hybrid Organizations

Hybrids are somewhat of a blend between nonprofits and for-profits, and may be legally incorporated as either type depending on a variety of factors. Social entrepreneurial organizations in their truest sense would fall into this category. A good example of a well-known hybrid organization is Goodwill Industries International, Inc., a nonprofit organization by legal status that operates for-profit business units (the Goodwill thrift stores) that employ people with barriers to employment. Such an organization definitely has certain profit targets that it must meet to sustain its commercial retail operations, but the organization also has a primary focus on its social mission. Some for-profit firms that choose social entrepreneurship as their guiding business model may also place mission first, but organize themselves as for-profit companies. Such for-profit companies make the conscious decision to forego some profit in order to achieve a social mission. A benefit corporation (for more details on this type of corporation, see www.bcorporation.net/) is a recently introduced legal designation for these types of companies that are for-profit but place emphasis on a social mission. Social work managers with a business mindset are certainly needed in these hybrid organizations. In my mind, hybrid organizations are indeed best served by having social work managers at the helm because social workers understand client and community situations and, with the help of some further training in some instances, can also do quite well with the business side of the operation.

Other Types of Organizations

Other organizational types that employ social work managers may include government agencies in which social work managers can work to improve service delivery in the public sector. A good example is public child welfare, a government industry that employs many social workers and social work managers in states and communities across the United States. Certain quasi-governmental organizations also exist, such as economic or neighborhood development entities dedicated to bettering entire communities or cities. Policy-oriented organizations, think tanks, advocacy groups, community organizations, and so forth might also be good avenues for social work managers with a keen macro interest wishing to effect social change at the policy level. Academic institutions and universities can also be possibilities for the social work manager to impart management and business knowledge to students and trainees— and to disseminate knowledge through writing articles and books on these topics.

Essential Business Skills for Social Work Managers: Key Domains

In short, this book is designed to prepare social work students to become social work managers and leaders in the human services, as well as to help junior to mid-level social work managers reach the top levels within this field. It is important to think of yourself as a business manager as well as a social worker in this context. Thinking in this manner may involve a focus on the balance between efficiency and effectiveness of your program's activities, or the development of a socially motivated profit orientation such that you manage your program or agency to earn a profit, or surplus, in order to reinvest the monetary gains back into the program or agency. This does not mean that your profit motive should be paramount as it would if you were running a for-profit business. Rather, you should manage for both mission and money, and strive for the "double-bottom line." Doing so will ensure greater sustainability of the essential programs and services offered to clients. Being businesslike can also manifest itself in other ways, such as presenting yourself professionally, strategically managing your professional relationships, communicating properly, succinctly, and transparently, and so forth.

This book focuses on the following core business domains of social work management, which complement other social work skill domains in the overall construct of social work management, as depicted in Figure 1.5: financial management, talent management, and the management of marketing, sales, and communications. It is my belief that once they are mastered, the business skills within these domains can augment the foundational social work skills learned in an undergraduate social work

Figure 1.5 Essential Social Work Management Skill Domains

program or an MSW program in order to achieve excellence in human services management. These are the types of skills one learns in a detailed manner during an MBA program. It is my hope that you can read this book in lieu of spending tens of thousands of dollars getting your MBA as I did, or at least these chapters will introduce you to the business side of social work management and spark your interest in furthering your professional education and development by taking training courses in specific domain areas in which you feel you need further development.

Chapter Summary

This chapter began with a practice example from my social work management experience highlighting the unpredictable yet opportunity-rich life of an executive in the human service industry. I discussed an occasion in which my business training helped me to effectively "sell" and represent my human service organization in public. In addition, this chapter included an introduction to the practice of social entrepreneurship—the blending of business skills with social work practice—designed to provide a contextual foundation for all of the content in this book. Further, the types of organizations in which social work managers are employed—nonprofit, for-profit, hybrid, and other organizations—as well as a brief case example of business-oriented social work management were included.

The important concepts from this chapter to be sure to understand before proceeding are as follows:

- Social work management has evolved in recent years to become more businesslike and entrepreneurial.
- Social entrepreneurship—a term used broadly to refer to businesslike social work management practice—is a growing phenomenon that combines business management skills with social work practice. Social enterprise, social venturing, social innovation, and so forth are similar concepts.
- Becoming businesslike is not easy for most social workers, but essential business skills can be learned during a degree program or afterward.
- Businesslike social work managers can find meaningful employment in an array of organizational types: nonprofit, for-profit, hybrid, and others.
- The essential social work management business skill domains, which complement social work skill domains, are: financial management, talent management, and the management of marketing, sales, and communications.

Suggested Learning Exercises

- Imagine that you meet a very influential person (e.g. an executive director or president of a large philanthropic foundation) while waiting in line at the supermarket and they ask you to tell them about your organization or program. (*Hint*: they may be able to provide substantial funding for one of your new projects!) With a partner in class, practice making a two-minute pitch for these types of occasions about the organization or program where you work or have your field placement. If possible, stand up in front of the class and deliver your two-minute pitch in front of your peers to practice it further. Practice is so important with the two-minute pitch!
- Perform a social work management skill inventory by exploring the three business skill domains of social work management as related to your work in the field: (1) financial management; (2) talent management; and (3) marketing, sales, and communications. Make a list of experiences you have had in each of these three categories. What were your strengths and weaknesses with

CHANGES IN SOCIAL WORK MANAGEMENT

regard to each experience? If you lack experiences in any category, make a list of relevant assignments that might be available to you in your work or field placement and discuss how you might involve yourself in these assignments.

- Find a social worker in your area of interest that you consider entrepreneurial. Set up an informational meeting or a phone call with this person and ask him or her to describe the type of work he or she does, how the work has evolved, how he or she learned to do this work, and what skills are most important to master. If possible, try to "shadow" this person for a day to fully observe the entrepreneurial experience.
- Identify social work managers or students (perhaps some of your classmates) that work in each of the following organizational categories: nonprofit, for-profit, hybrid, and other. Ask them about their experiences managing programs and projects. Compare and contrast the experiences of those working in different types of organizations.

Internet Resources

The Network for Social Work Management (NSWM)—a global membership organization dedicated to advancing social work management practice and scholarship in the areas of health and human services. The Network hosts a popular annual conference, sponsors the academic journal *Human Service Organizations: Management, Leadership & Governance* (www.tandfonline.com/toc/wasw20/current), hosts free webinars on various management topics, provides mentorship opportunities, and also publishes on its website a set of competencies for human service managers, some of which align with the main concepts of this book: www.socialworkmanager.org.

Association for Community Organization and Social Administration (ACOSA)—an international membership organization for community organizers, activists, nonprofit administrators, community builders, policy practitioners, students, and educators. ACOSA sponsors the *Journal of Community Practice* (www.tandfonline.com/toc/wcom20/current). In addition, the organization, mainly via its website and newsletter, disseminates timely information on innovations in community and administrative practice, as well as providing a variety of opportunities for networking and professional advancement: www.acosa.org.

Ashoka—a global organization supporting and promoting the work of social entrepreneurs and "changemakers" focused on solving complex social problems through innovation and entrepreneurship: www. ashoka.org.

The Social Innovation Fund (SIF)—a project of the U.S. Federal Government's Corporation for National and Community Service (www.national service.gov), SIF, established in 2009, awards grants for innovative solutions to pressing problems faced by individuals, families, and communities across the United States.

Stanford Social Innovation Review—a scholarly magazine and website published by the Stanford Center on Philanthropy and Civil Society (http://pacscenter.stanford.edu) at Stanford University, which includes cutting-edge articles on entrepreneurship and innovation in the social sector: www.ssireview.org.

Social Enterprise Alliance—a U.S.-based membership, networking, and technical assistance organization for aspiring and practicing social entrepreneurs: www.se-alliance.org.

New Jersey Social Innovation Institute—a unique training program for nascent social entrepreneurs and a symposia series sponsored by Rutgers Business School-Newark and New Brunswick: www.njsesummit.org.

Center for Social Innovation—located at the Graduate School of Social Work at Boston College, this is one of the few centers dedicated to social innovation that is housed within a social work educational institution. The center offers the Social Innovation Lab, an incubator-type program for social service organizations, as well as various symposia on innovation topics and an array of helpful resources available on its website: www.bc.edu/content/bc/schools/gssw/csi.html.

The Alliance for Nonprofit Management—a U.S.-based community of capacity builders in the nonprofit sector, which sponsors an annual conference with training workshops and presentations: http://thealliance conference.org.

American Public Human Services Association—a U.S.-based, nationwide membership organization representing state and local-level human service agencies through their top-level leadership. The website contains various resources that would be helpful to social work managers working in a variety of fields within the public sector: www.aphsa.org.

Notes

1. Contains excerpts from Germak and Singh's 2010 article, "Social entrepreneurship: Changing the way social workers do business," *Administration in Social Work*, *34*(1): 79–95, reprinted by permission of the publisher.
2. In order to maintain the confidentiality of this individual and her organization, her name has been changed. She is an MSW-level social worker employed as a program manager in the human services arena.

2
FINANCIAL MANAGEMENT

The decision to include a chapter on financial management as the first in a series of essential skills chapters in this book was a deliberate one. The healthy finances of any organization, whether a for-profit company, a nonprofit human service agency, or a government entity, are the building blocks upon which an organization can successfully carry out its mission. Moreover, without adequate oversight and prudent management of finances, an organization of any type may not properly allocate its resources and, ultimately, the organization may need to close its doors due to fiscal mismanagement. This logic also holds true for individual programs in addition to entire organizations—if the money is not managed appropriately, it is difficult for a program to be effective. Perhaps most importantly, for many social work managers financial management is not something that comes easily, and therefore this chapter is meant to serve as an introduction to understanding and managing the finances of a social work program or organization in order to alleviate some of the common frustrations.

This chapter will examine what social work managers need to know in order to get the finances in order of a social work program or organization, and maintain a healthy financial environment in which a program or organization can effectively carry out its mission. The level of detail in this chapter is appropriate for social work managers and not necessarily for chief financial officers or budget office managers. Such individuals would be best served by an advanced and comprehensive text on financial or managerial accounting. The orientation of this chapter is appropriate for non-financially inclined social work managers.

To develop an understanding of the various aspects of financial management that are essential for social work managers, this chapter will begin with an overview of the commonly used financial statements or reports that social work managers encounter in their work. Next, I will discuss how managers can project, or estimate, revenues and expenses in order to better plan for the future. This will include an explanation of annualizing expenses and revenues, and an introduction to "pro forma" financial statements and financial modeling. Furthermore, there is a section on capital structure (the means by which programs and organizations are financed) common to nonprofit human service organizations. Importantly, most of the concepts covered in this chapter are universal; they can be applied to both nonprofit and for-profit ventures, albeit with some differences in terminology. Public-sector financial management is a somewhat different process and not really the focus of this chapter, although some concepts may cross over and be helpful to public sector professionals.

The Importance of Financial Health

In the corporate world, financial objectives are paramount for an organization's survival. Stockholders of public companies—those firms that sell shares of their stock to the public—demand that the management team maintain and enhance profitability and create economic value for the firm and for stockholders. In the world of commercial business, when a company is not financially healthy, serious problems ensue, the results of which often include bankruptcy filings and major restructuring of the company's core operations.

The focus on financial health is no less important in the nonprofit world. There is a common phrase well known by most social work managers and leaders of nonprofit human service organizations—"no money, no mission." The meaning of this expression is self-evident. However, it bears noting that social work managers should pay special attention to financial management to avoid such a predicament. In social work, unlike other areas of the nonprofit sector such as the arts, for example, inadequate financial management, or a "no money, no mission" predicament could mean the difference between an organization's clients receiving services or going without essential programs and services. In some extreme cases, this could represent a life-or-death scenario for clients.

No Money, No Mission: Social work managers must manage finances appropriately. Otherwise it is not possible to successfully carry out the mission of a human service program or organization.

Figure 2.1 Key Point

Thus, I argue that the first thing a social work manager should attend to is the financial health of the program or organization in which he or she works. Prudent financial management is especially critical in entrepreneurial social work programs or organizations, as described in Chapter 1 in the discussion on social entrepreneurship. In such situations, earning a surplus is an important aspect of the overall mission allowing for sustainability of programs and services.

Nonetheless, I suggest that such a *finances first* mentality will allow social work managers the flexibility to not only achieve a mission, but also create a truly transformative organization for all stakeholders —employees, clients, community members, and so forth. It may be helpful to think of the finances of your program or organization as an intricate structure, such as a house, in which all parts are interconnected and necessary to make a whole. Just as you would not live in a house without a roof, for instance, you would not operate a social work program without a basic budget, financial statements, or a comprehensive understanding of the other important financial parts that make the program whole.

Understanding the Financial Health of Your Program or Organization

Whether you are an MSW intern, a program supervisor, a director, or an agency executive, you will, at some point in your career as a social work manager, need to analyze and interpret financial data pertaining to your program or organization. Being able to do this is important because, as mentioned above, the financial condition of your program or organization could mean, in the extreme case, the difference between clients receiving services or not.

At the program or project level, there are budgets, which are essentially financial descriptions of how a program or project will be implemented as per a grant, contract, or some other directive from the organization's management. Budgets are prospective documents that seek to describe a program's present performance and predict future revenue and expense (Kettner, Moroney, & Martin, 2008). Budgets come in many types and formats (Kettner, 2002), and should quite simply include a list of all revenue that comes into a program or project and all expenses that will be incurred by the program or project. There is little standardization as to how budgets are presented; different organizations use different software programs and formats to present budgets. Additionally, budgets can be prepared manually in a spreadsheet program such as Microsoft Excel. Because of this lack of standardization, I will not discuss basic budgeting preparation per se, but rather will focus on the more standardized financial statements that social work managers must be able to read, analyze, interpret, and explain: the balance sheet, the income statement, and the statement of cash flows. Still, the subsequent discussion of projecting revenue and expense should help you create budgets for your program or project in whatever format your organization requires. A sample budget template is provided in Figure 2.2 for your use in the budgeting process.

Basics of Nonprofit Accounting

Before explaining the first standardized financial statement, the balance sheet, it is important to introduce you to the basic accounting equation, which is used in all businesses—both for-profit and nonprofit—to understand how the various facets of financial claims and obligations

FINANCIAL MANAGEMENT

EXPENSE TYPE	ESTIMATED EXPENSE ($)	COMMENTS
Personnel Services (PS)		
Total PS		
Other than Personnel Services (OTPS)		
Total OTPS		
Grand Total (PS + OTPS)		

Figure 2.2 Budget Template

interact and ultimately manifest themselves in the balance sheet. Figure 2.3 outlines the accounting equation, a simple formula that states that an organization's assets must equal the sum of its liabilities and net assets. This equation holds true for all types of organizations (Horngren, Sundem, & Elliott, 2002). Although the components of the equation

---

$$\text{ASSETS (A)} = \text{LIABILITIES (L)} + \text{NET ASSETS (NA)}$$

Figure 2.3 The Nonprofit Accounting Equation

may vary between organizations, there must always be a balance between assets on the one hand, and liabilities and net assets on the other.

You may be wondering at this point what exactly are assets, liabilities, and net assets. Figure 2.4 provides definitions of these three concepts. Essentially, assets are anything that an organization owns or for which it can make a claim. Examples of assets would be any property that an agency owns. For example, supportive housing organizations often own apartments or buildings in which clients are housed. These buildings are considered assets of the agency because, conceivably, the agency owns these properties. (On the other hand, the clients living in the building are not assets of the agency; people—whether they are clients, employees, etc.—cannot be owned or claimed.) Other examples of assets would be any cash or investments that an organization owns, plus accounts receivable, which is an accounting term for payments that have not yet been delivered for a service or product that an organization has provided—these accounts have yet to be received by the organization and are therefore considered assets because the organization can make a claim for these funds. Collection agencies, for example, work on behalf of organizations to collect accounts receivable that may be in arrears.

Liabilities, on the other hand, are not items that are owned by the organization, but rather are things to which someone else (or some other organization) can lay claim. Examples of organizational liabilities would

---

Assets are what an organization owns or claims. Examples are cash, accounts receivable, vehicles, furniture, property, and so forth.

Liabilities are what someone (or something) else owns or claims. Examples are accounts payable, wages or benefits payable, loans outstanding, pension commitments, and so forth.

Net Assets represent the difference between assets and liabilities. Healthy organizations have a positive value for net assets – more assets than liabilities.

Figure 2.4 Assets, Liabilities, and Net Assets

be any accounts that are payable to others, such as wages that are owed to employees but have not yet been paid out, loans that an organization has taken from financial institutions to pay for necessary equipment but not yet paid off, and so forth. In these examples, parties outside of the organization can claim ownership of each of the items.

Assets and liabilities are interrelated, and it is a useful exercise to think about how they are related. For instance, an important relationship between assets and liabilities is that for every liability that an organization holds, another entity can claim this liability as an asset in its portfolio. Loans, for example, taken out by an organization to finance a fleet of agency vehicles would be a liability to the agency that took out the loan because the agency must pay this loan back over time; the agency does not own the loan in the sense that the money was given to the organization, as is also the case with a donation or grant. Conversely, the bank that made the loan to the agency can count that loan amount as an asset, technically a loan receivable, in its portfolio because it will be paid back by the agency, and the bank can therefore lay claim to this amount of money plus interest in most cases.

Finally, net assets are simply the difference between the sum totals of a nonprofit organization's assets and its liabilities. The concept of net assets is unique to nonprofit accounting. In for-profits, this component of the accounting equation, called *owners' equity*, is more complex and involves the various layers of firm ownership that are held by shareholders or other owners of the firm. In fact, for for-profit organizations, this issue of owners' equity is so important that a key financial statement, the statement of owners' equity, is used in addition to the three financial statements germane to nonprofit organizations that I describe here.

Fortunately, in nonprofit accounting, we do not need to worry about issues of owners' equity. It is sufficient to know that most nonprofit organizations have assets that outweigh liabilities to some degree— positive net assets. This is an important concept because if such an organization for some extreme reason needed to go out of business, it would be able to pay off all of its liabilities, which are most likely legal obligations, and then wind down its business. On the other hand, an unhealthy organization would have more liabilities than assets in its portfolio—negative net assets. According to Zietlow, Hankin, and

32   FINANCIAL MANAGEMENT

Seidner (2007), this is a problematic situation and such an organization is at great risk of not being able to meet its financial obligations in the event of an emergency.

The Balance Sheet

The balance sheet is a snapshot of an organization's financial position—the actual amounts of all of its assets and liabilities—at a given point in time. Because the balance sheet is a picture of an organization's finances at a point in time, it is sometimes referred to as the statement of financial position. Figure 2.5 is a typical balance sheet in a format that shows the financial position of an agency at two points in time—June 30, 2011 and June 30, 2012. It is customary to show two yearly periods in the balance sheet document so trends can be noted and analyzed between yearly periods. In the case of Figure 2.5, the points in time are at the end of the fiscal year for two fiscal year periods. Note that in this sample balance sheet, the accounting equation holds true for both years—the assets of the organization equal the sum of the organization's liabilities and its net assets. This rule must hold true for all balance sheets that this organization produces. In future balance sheets, there will most likely be changes in the value of assets, liabilities, and net assets, but both sides of the accounting equation must remain in balance. If this is not the case, there is probably an error in accounting and you should take time to review all items in the balance sheet to make sure they are correctly represented.

In addition, you can tell that the organization behind this balance sheet is in a relatively healthy financial situation. The way you can quickly determine this is by looking at the amount of total assets and total liabilities for both years. In both cases, the amount of assets outweighs the amount of liabilities by nearly two to one. This tells you that the organization could liquidate (sell) its assets in the event of some financial catastrophe and pay off its liabilities two times over. Thus, we would say that the organization represented here is financially healthy. Likewise, look at the amount of cash and the amount of accrued wages for each year. The cash amount is significantly higher, which tells us that this organization could pay its employees from its bank account more than two times over if a crisis were to hit. This is more evidence that the organization represented here is in good financial health.

FINANCIAL MANAGEMENT   33

	June 30, 2012	June 30, 2011
Assets		
Cash	$ 856,922	$ 754,998
Investments	23,456	22,875
Accounts Receivable	123,450	103,546
Prepaid Expenses	45,657	49,765
Property, Plant, & Equipment	1,245,458	1,215,564
Total Assets	2,294,943	2,146,748
Liabilities		
Accounts Payable	$ 175,234	$150,555
Accrued Wages & Benefits	368,987	322,335
Loans Outstanding	220,345	235,556
Deferred Revenue	295,479	305,386
Total Liabilities	1,060,045	1,013,832
Net Assets	$ 1,234,898	$ 1,132,916

Figure 2.5 Sample Year-End Balance Sheet

The Income Statement

Although very important in communicating the financial health of an
organization at any point in time, the balance sheet does not tell us
anything about, during a given time period, the amount or type of
revenue coming in to an organization or program, or about the amount
or type of expense being incurred by an organization or program. Thus,
the income statement, the next standardized financial statement used in
all of business, fills this gap.

The income statement always represents a particular period of time
and lists all revenues received during that period and expenses incurred.
At the bottom of the income statement, the amount of net income is

listed. This is the amount of profit (positive net income) or loss (negative net income) that was realized during the period. You calculate net income by subtracting the total amount of expenses from the total amount of revenue for a particular period. Net income is often referred to as the bottom line, which literally means the amount of profit or loss listed on the bottom-most line of the income statement.

Figure 2.6 is a sample quarterly income statement for the three-month period of April 1, 2012 through June 30, 2012. Although income statements can be generated for any period, even daily if desired, it is most customary in nonprofit human service organizations for managers to review and analyze income statements on a quarterly (every three months) basis. In fact, most of the for-profit world revolves around quarterly income statements, too. If you have ever read about Wall Street

	April 1, 2012 through June 30, 2012
Income	
Grants	$ 575,500
Other Donations	7,150
Event Revenue	1,125
Fee-for-Service	223,550
Sale of Products	565
Total Income	807,890
Expense	
Personnel Services (PS)	$ 674,322
Other than Personnel Services (OTPS)	105,677
Miscellaneous Operating	12,575
Total Expense	792,574
Net Income	$ 15,316

Figure 2.6 Sample Three-Month Income Statement

analysts predicting quarterly earnings for companies, what they are doing in part is actually trying to predict what the net income will be for a given company at the end of a given quarter.

As Figure 2.6 illustrates, during this three-month period the organization or program performed quite well by producing a positive net income of $15,316. This amount is the total profit or surplus that was generated after all expenses were taken into account. This positive surplus can thus be reinvested into the program or redistributed to another program of the agency if allowed. Another key point to glean from this sample income statement is the high proportion of personnel services (PS) to overall income. Nearly 83 percent of this program's revenue was taken up by wages and benefits to staff ($674,322 divided by $807,890). This is not uncommon to nonprofit human service organizations, for example. Social work is a service business (this will be discussed in more detail in Chapter 3) and labor costs are naturally the highest expense in social work program budgets. Contrarily, manufacturing companies typically have higher raw materials and supplies costs—these are known as other than personnel services (OTPS) expenses—rather than PS expenses.

It is important to note that, historically, in the nonprofit sector, the income statement was not used as often as the "statement of functional expenses." In fact, many nonprofit agencies still report a statement of functional expenses in their annual reports, audited financial statements, and as part of the Form 990 report, which is an informational return document required each year in the United States by the Internal Revenue Service. The statement of functional expenses, although important as it lists all of the expenses incurred by an organization, communicates almost nothing about revenues generated by an organization. In my view, the longtime reliance on the statement of functional expenses reinforces the idea that nonprofits should not earn a profit and that net income is a concept that should be discussed only in the for-profit sector. However, I argue that nonprofits, especially in the human services, need to pay attention to revenues and should strive for positive net income, the profit from which can be reinvested into programs and services.

The Statement of Cash Flows

The third standardized financial statement that is used in nonprofit organizational accounting is the statement of cash flows. Cash monitoring is so important to social work managers because most of the programs and organizations in which we work have almost no "cash cushion" in the event that cash is mishandled or, as sometimes unfortunately occurs, embezzled or misappropriated. Even in the rare cases where programs or agencies are flush with cash, the misuse of cash could mean the difference in clients receiving certain specialty services, the amount of hours programs can operate, the number of staff available for clients, and so forth.

The flow of cash both in and out of an agency or program happens all the time, and it is nearly impossible for a busy social work manager to keep track of the flow of cash without the help of a summary statement. Summarizing the flow of cash is essentially what the statement of cash flows does. Note that cash is listed on the balance sheet (see the top line in Figure 2.5), but from the balance sheet in Figure 2.5, for instance, we have no idea how the cash balance went from $754,998 on June 30, 2011 to $856,922 on June 30, 2012. Therefore, we can look to the statement of cash flows (see Figure 2.7) to help us understand how and why the cash balance changed (Figures 2.5 and 2.7 represent the same fictitious organization).

	7/1/11–6/30/12	7/1/10–6/30/11
Net Cash from Operations	$ 112,218	$ 251,131
Net Cash from Investing	5,456	(24,595)
Net Cash from Financing	(15,750)	(17,530)
Net Change in Cash Over Period	101,924	209,006
Cash Beginning of Period	754,998	545,992
Cash End of Period	856,922	754,998

Figure 2.7 Sample Year-End Statement of Cash Flows

FINANCIAL MANAGEMENT   37

Similar to the logic behind the income statement, the statement of cash flows is always presented over a period of time. In Figure 2.7, the sample statement of cash flows is presented on a yearly basis in order to correspond to the sample balance sheet presented in Figure 2.5. It is customary for a balance sheet to be accompanied by a statement of cash flows so that the cash line on the balance sheet can be better understood.

From Figure 2.7, we can see that the net change in cash from July 1, 2011 through June 30, 2012 for this particular organization was $101,924. At first glance, we can tell that this organization increased its cash position, which is typically a good sign, but we need to dig a bit deeper to understand how this happened. Thus, we look at the following three categories of the statement of cash flows: cash from operations, cash from investing, and cash from financing. In order to simplify this concept, which is probably new to you, Figure 2.7 only lists net cash from operations, investing, and financing over the two one-year periods. Note that each category—operations, investing, and financing—in reality can have many sub-categories to support the final, net numbers listed in Figure 2.7.

Still, it is sufficient to understand that cash from operations includes all cash that was spent to make the program or organization run, including staff salaries, rent payments for program space, and so forth. The cash from operations category also includes cash that was received, such as grants to the organization or income earned from other program or commercial activities. The final number that gets included on the statement of cash flows for this category—the net cash from operations figure—is the amount of cash received minus the amount of cash expended on operating activities. In a healthy program or organization, net cash from operations would be positive—more money was taken in than was expended.

Additionally, cash from investing would include such activities as the organization's purchases of new equipment, vehicles, real estate, stocks, and so forth, as well as any proceeds from the sale of such short- or long-term investments. These activities represent revenue and expenses that fall outside of the day-to-day operations of the organization but do involve the flow of cash in and out of the agency. Similar to the logic behind net cash from operations, the net cash from investing amount would be the amount of cash received minus the amount of cash expended. Note that in Figure 2.7, there is a negative number in this category for the first year and a positive number in the second. This may mean that the organization made significant purchases of equipment, for instance in the first year represented, resulting in a negative cash balance, then made sales of equipment or other investments in the second year, which resulted in a surplus of cash—a positive net value for cash from investing.

Finally, the financing category of the statement of cash flows includes all activities the organization engaged in related to financing its activities, usually by use of credit, loans, and so forth. The organization represented by Figure 2.7 may have used lines of credit to meet its payroll obligations or had interest payments due on mortgage loans for properties it owns. In nonprofit organizations, financing activities are almost always indicated by cash flowing out of the organization—negative net cash from financing. It is very rare that nonprofit organizations make loans or serve as creditors, thereby receiving payments and having positive financing balances. Moreover, it is not uncommon to see zero activity in the financing category for nonprofit organizations because they do not typically expend or receive cash in this manner. In most cases, therefore, the amount for net cash from financing would be negative or zero.

Projecting Revenue and Expense

Thus far, this chapter has explored how to retroactively analyze an entity's financial situation by way of the balance sheet, income statement, and statement of cash flows. These financial statements tell us what happened in the past with regard to finances. However, it is just as important for social work managers to know how to predict how finances will behave in the future. This concept is referred to as projecting or forecasting, and should become a key part of your financial management toolkit. For example, most funders these days require a projection of program expenses as part of your proposal, which will show the funder how you predict the funding will be spent. Likewise, as will be discussed in Chapter 5, business planning has become quite popular in human service programs, and investors want to know your predictions on future revenue as well as expenses. Importantly, as you project revenue and expense,

FINANCIAL MANAGEMENT 39

keep in mind that projections are always estimates of reality. There is no way to know for certain how much revenue will come in or exactly what your expenses will be. To deal with this uncertainty, there are certain best practice techniques for revenue and expense projection, including annualizing, as described henceforth.

Annualizing Revenue and Expense

One of the quickest, easiest, and often most reliable ways of projecting both revenue and expense is through a process called annualizing. Basically, when an amount of money is annualized, the amount, often a smaller amount, is converted into a larger, yearly amount that can then be used to compile a projected annual budget for a particular program or activity. With this projected, annual amount, you can not only build pro forma financial statements (discussed in next section), but also you can see the financial impact of a program in its larger entirety. Let us look at some examples of how this works.

Imagine that you are a manager in charge of a social service program and have been asked by your supervisor to predict next year's fee-for-service revenue based on the first three months of this year (you have a three-month income statement that lists this revenue amount). Following the steps outlined in Figure 2.8, n would equal 3 because the information you have available is a revenue amount for a period of three months.

Expense/Revenue Amount a for Period of n Months	Multiplier				Expense/Revenue Amount A for Period of 12 Months
$n = 1$	a	$\times$	12	$=$	A
2	a	$\times$	6	$=$	A
3	a	$\times$	4	$=$	A
4	a	$\times$	3	$=$	A
6	a	$\times$	2	$=$	All

Figure 2.8 One-Step Annualizing

40 FINANCIAL MANAGEMENT

Let us use the three-month fee-for-service revenue amount from Figure 2.6, $223,500, which would be the value of a. Therefore, following Figure 2.8, you would multiply $223,550 by 4, which would yield $894,200. Thus, you could tell your supervisor that you have annualized three months of fee-for-service revenue from this year to project an annual fee-for-service revenue amount of $894,200 for next year. This would be a reliable estimate of next year's revenue in this category based on a process of one-step annualizing.

Let us imagine that your supervisor is satisfied with this answer and can tell that you have based your analysis on sound logic, but she needs an additional piece of information. She says that she is looking at a report of five months of salary data for your program (the five-month total amount is $202,277) and is concerned about what the total salary amount might be for next year. She asks you to estimate this amount and get back to her so she can put it into her master budget.

This task will involve a two-step annualizing process as outlined in Figure 2.9. In this case, n equals 5 and a equals $202,277. Therefore, to arrive at a reliable projection for next year's annual salary expense, you will first need to derive your current monthly salary cost by dividing

Expense/ Revenue Amount a for Period of n Months			Divisor			Expense/ Revenue Amount a_1 for Period of 1 Month		Multiplier		Expense/ Revenue Amount A for Period of 12 Months
$n =$	5	a	$\div$	5	$=$	a_1	$\times$	12	$=$	A
	7	a	$\div$	7	$=$	a_1	$\times$	12	$=$	A
	8	a	$\div$	8	$=$	a_1	$\times$	12	$=$	A
	9	a	$\div$	9	$=$	a_1	$\times$	12	$=$	A
	10	a	$\div$	10	$=$	a_1	$\times$	12	$=$	A
	11	a	$\div$	11	$=$	a_1	$\times$	12	$=$	A

Figure 2.9 Two-Step Annualizing

FINANCIAL MANAGEMENT 41

$202,277 by 5, which yields $40,455 rounded to the nearest dollar. The second step would be to multiply this monthly expense by 12 to arrive at a projected annual expense amount. The amount of this calculation is $484,460 ($40,455 multiplied by 12). Therefore, you can tell your supervisor that your projection of next year's total salary expense for your program based on annualizing data from this year will be $484,460.

Building Pro Forma Financial Statements

As you proceed to compiling more complex projections of revenue and expense for a program or an organization, you will be asked to put together what are called pro forma financial statements. Essentially, pro forma statements are versions of the three core financial statements— balance sheet, income statement, and statement of cash flows—that are not only based on past events, but also contain estimates of future financial data. The process of creating pro forma financial statements is often referred to as financial statement modeling, which is in and of itself a career path within the financial services industry, for example. There are people working in banks and investment houses that specialize in building financial models and nothing else! Thus, my aim in this book is to introduce you to this practice while realizing that to become truly expert in modeling, one needs to devote significant time and attention to it. Still, social work managers can benefit from knowing how to construct simple models of financial statements.

Figure 2.10 illustrates a pro forma income statement (the first column contains data from the three-month income statement from Figure 2.6), which estimates both revenue and expense for four quarters (one year) going forward from the end of the fourth quarter of 2012 (June 30), which is that last known data point for this particular organization. Consequently, the shaded columns on this income statement are the projections of what is expected going forward into the future. When building pro forma financial statements, it is customary to show known data followed by your projections so that the reader can see how your projections relate to the known data, and the basis upon which you are making your estimates.

I would like to explore a few of the income and expense lines from Figure 2.10 so that you understand the logic used in building this

	Q4–12	Q1–13	Q2–13	Q3–13	Q4–13
Income ($)					
Grants	575,000	592,765	592,765	592,765	592,765
Other Donations	7,150	7,150	7,865	6,559	7,293
Event Revenue	1,125	0	0	0	1,181
Fee-for-Service	223,550	228,021	232,581	237,233	241,977
Sale of Products	565	581	599	617	635
Total Income	807,890	828,518	833,810	837,175	843,852
Expense ($)					
Personnel Services (PS)	674,322	714,781	714,781	714,781	714,781
OTPS	105,677	107,790	107,790	107,790	107,790
Miscellaneous Operating	12,575	12,826	13,083	13,344	13,611
Total Expense	792,574	835,398	835,654	835,916	836,183
Net Income ($)	15,316	–6,880	–1,844	1,258	7,669

Figure 2.10 Sample Four-Quarter Pro Forma Income Statement

particular financial model. Remember that each pro forma financial statement will contain projections based on assumptions and contextual data for the specific organization or program at hand. Still, some of the logic used here may also apply to other situations in your work or field placement.

First, the projected amount of income from grants (Figure 2.10) jumps from $575,500 (last known data point) to $592,765 for Q1-13 and remains at that level for the entire fiscal year. This may be based on past history of grant revenue for this organization. It could be that grants are renewed during the first quarter of each year and do not change until the next fiscal year. The increased amount of $592,765 could be based on some information that has been communicated to this organization; the organization may have been informed by its funders that its grants would most likely increase by 3 percent and therefore this is sufficient information to make a reliable projection of grant revenue.

In addition, Figure 2.10 shows that fee-for-service revenue is expected to increase by 2 percent each quarter during the next fiscal year. This may be based on past trends of this type of revenue. However, unlike grants that are based on contractual arrangements between parties, fee-for-service revenue is more often variable. If clients for whatever reason opt out of services, or there is an unexpected surge in services, this 2 percent projection could be off base. Still, it is important to make a projection of some sort in a pro forma statement, and thus relying on past trends is a viable option.

Similarly, miscellaneous operating expense in Figure 2.10 is also predicted to increase by 2 percent each quarter during the subsequent fiscal year. From the data we have available, it is unclear how this estimate was made, but it should be based on some known, or relatively known, information about these expenses. As with the fee-for-service income, typically organizations base projections on prior trends, which to the best of their knowledge should predict future trends. Still, it is important to remember that projections are always uncertain; you can never predict with complete certainty how the finances of an organization or program will look into the future.

Understanding Nonprofit Capital Structure

Capital structure is a concept that is common to all companies, both for-profit and nonprofit, and pertains to the ways in which an organization is capitalized, or funded. Many for-profit companies have a distinct capital structure, in that they can sell stock to the public thereby providing financing for some of their activities. Nonprofits, on the other hand, cannot issue stock, but can receive grants, take out loans, earn income through related or unrelated business, and so forth. Understanding the common ways in which nonprofit human service organizations are capitalized will be helpful to understanding what may be the most feasible financing options for sustaining programs or starting new ones.

44 FINANCIAL MANAGEMENT

Table 2.1 Example of Nonprofit Human Service Organization Capital Structure

Type of Financing	Percentage of Total Financing
Government grants	55
Foundation grants	12
Fee-for-service	9
Corporate donations	8
Individual donations	6
Events	4
Lines of credit	3
Investments	2
Related/unrelated business	1

Table 2.1 outlines a typical nonprofit capital structure for a human service organization. Note that grants, both government and foundation, are the most common source of financing for this nonprofit organization. In this case, government grants plus foundation grants amount to 67 percent of the organization's total funding. This is fairly average, but some human service nonprofit organizations can be as much as 100 percent funded by grants. Few are funded minimally by grants. In addition to grants, fee-for-service income, most often encompassing Medicaid revenue in nonprofit human service organizations, is also a key component of the typical capital structure of an organization.

Outside of government grants, foundation grants, and fee-for-service income, nonprofit human service organizations, as illustrated by Table 2.1, usually are financed by smaller amounts of donations, event revenue, lines of credit, investment returns, and earned income from business endeavors. As noted in Chapter 1, this mix of revenue is starting to change in certain organizations as the traditional government and foundation grants become harder to obtain and sustain. The skills learned in this chapter with regard to financial statement analysis and estimation should prove useful as the capital structure landscape changes in the human services and there becomes much more variability in the manner through which nonprofit human service organizations and programs, for instance, are funded.

Chapter Summary

This chapter introduced what is arguably the most essential business skill for social work managers: managing the finances of a social work program or organization. I began with an overview of the nonprofit accounting equation and discussed definitions and examples of assets, liabilities, and net assets. Next, the three key financial statements for social work managers working in nonprofit human service organizations were explained. The balance sheet, or statement of financial position, illustrates the financial condition of a program or organization at a specific point in time. The income statement shows all revenue and expense related to a given entity occurring over a specified time period. Lastly, the statement of cash flows indicates the movement of cash both in and out of a program or organization during a certain time frame. This chapter also included a discussion of using annualizing techniques to project revenue and expense, as well as instructions on how to model pro forma financial statements. The chapter concluded with a discussion of capital structure in the nonprofit human services.

The important concepts from this chapter to be sure to understand are as follows:

- Proper financial oversight and management can ensure that clients of human service programs and organizations receive adequate and necessary services.
- The accounting equation used in nonprofit organizations is: Assets = Liabilities + Net Assets.
- The balance sheet, income statement, and statement of cash flows are the three standardized financial statements used in nonprofit human service programs. Social work managers should be comfortable analyzing and interpreting all of these statements.
- Projecting revenue and expense is a key skill, however there is always uncertainty involved with making projections.
- Nonprofit human service organizations have a distinct capital structure from that of for-profit firms, although the nature and mix of this capital structure is evolving.

Suggested Learning Exercises

- Make lists of all assets and liabilities that you think exist at your organization where you are employed or where you do your field placement. Then, obtain the balance sheet for your organization (this may be challenging if you are not privy to your organization's financial information, but keep at it and try to obtain the balance sheet!) and compare your list to what you see on the balance sheet. Are you surprised by anything you see on the balance sheet? Do you have anything listed that is not on the balance sheet? Why might this be?
- Write down all of the categories of income and expense that you think exist in your program where you work or are doing your field placement. Then, try to obtain an income statement for the program. How do your categories compare to the income statement? Are you struck by any of the income or expense amounts you see in the income statement?
- Based on the income statement obtained, create a pro forma income statement for the next period based on reasonable assumptions (use the same format for your statement as used in Figure 2.10). Think about how and why certain income or expense categories may increase or decrease and capture these estimates in your financial model.
- Investigate the capital structure of your organization (you may need to ask someone in the finance office for information on this) and list each component of the structure with its estimated percentage of total financing as in Table 2.1. What does your organization's capital structure tell you about its financial health? How would you suggest improving the capital structure?

Internet Resources

Nonprofit Accounting Basics—a project of the Greater Washington Society of Certified Public Accountants, this online resource includes a wealth of technical information for those seeking more depth in accounting concepts geared toward the nonprofit sector: www.nonprofitaccounting basics.org.

FINANCIAL MANAGEMENT

Accounting Coach—a robust online resource that aims to provide a wealth of information about all aspects of general accounting for free to the public: www.accountingcoach.com.

The Center on Budget and Policy Priorities—a leading policy organization based in Washington, DC, which produces research reports and other tools to help social work managers and others understand public sector budget issues at the U.S. federal and state levels: http://cbpp.org.

Nonprofit Finance Fund—a financial advisory firm focused on the nonprofit sector, which publishes the annual "State of the Sector" survey (http://nonprofitfinancefund.org/state-of-the-sector-surveys) on the financial health of the nonprofit sector in the United States: www.non profitfinancefund.org.

Financial Management Resources for Nonprofits—the National Council of Nonprofits (www.councilofnonprofits.org) hosts on its website an expansive listing of nonprofit financial management tools, tips, and resource articles, including those related to budgeting, financial policies, cash flow issues, and internal control practices: www.councilofnon profits.org/resources/financial-management.

Beginner's Guide to Financial Statements—a free resource published by the U.S. Securities and Exchange Commission with basic information on how to read financial statements: balance sheets, income statements, and so forth. This resource is geared toward understanding the financial statements of for-profit companies, but learning the financial jargon can also be helpful for understanding nonprofit or public-sector finance and accounting concepts: www.sec.gov/investor/pubs/begfinstmtguide.htm.

Resources for Nonprofit Financial Management—the website of the Wallace Foundation includes a library of free resources—articles, tem-plates, and sample financial policies and statements—aimed at helping nonprofit organizations become and remain financially healthy: www.wallacefoundation.org/knowledge-center/Resources-for-Financial-Management/Pages/default.aspx.

3

TALENT MANAGEMENT

In my view, the overall talent base of a human service organization includes not only the organization's staff members, but also its volunteers, student interns, board members, strategic partners, and anyone that helps the organization carry out its mission—sometimes even its clients. Talent is a term used by many progressively managed and led for-profit companies because it is more empowering to refer to an organization's human resources—the people that work for and with an organization—in this manner. The word, talent, also sounds more palatable to an organization's employees; they are not just a human resource used by the organization, but can offer the organization something of value—their talents. In fact, depending on the type of services provided by a human service organization, clients may also be considered talent. An example of this would be a social work advocacy organization that employs its service beneficiaries as spokespeople and advocates for the causes championed by the organization. Thus, talent is a broad but appropriate way of describing the human resource aspects of a human service organization.

Still, as with all aspects of social work, there is a suggested prioritization to what social work managers should focus on in their work, and thus I purport that managing the talent of a program or organization would be toward the top of the list, but not the ultimate first priority. I know this might sound surprising to some social workers, but financial management, as explored in Chapter 2, should still be first priority on this list, quickly followed by the management of talent—employees, boards of directors, volunteers, networks, and so forth—as the next biggest priority, which is the topic of this third chapter.

The reason for this prioritization is that it does take proper financial management skills and budgeting acumen to be able to effectively manage the human side of a program or organization—there is no talent that comes at zero cost to an organization. Some may argue that an organization's staff members, for example, should come first no matter what else may be on the priority list, or that clients must be the top priority in any social work agency regardless of other agency responsibilities. I agree with this empowering notion in principle, yet it does often take astute financial planning in the human service sector to be able to put your people first and to provide quality services for clients. By following this prioritization, the social work manager is able to provide more resources to the people that work for and benefit from an organization.

This chapter will begin with a brief practice example related to how social work managers must often balance financial concerns with talent management. A discussion of social work as a service business will follow this example. The chapter then continues with a presentation of strategies for talent management in all directions: downward, upward, and sideways, including an interview with a social work manager that illustrates the use of some of these strategies in the effective management and development of a nonprofit human service organization's board of directors.

Practice Example: Balancing Financial and Talent Management

It was that dreaded time of year again at our nonprofit human service organization: health insurance policy renewal season. The organization's health insurance agent was coming to meet with me to give me the update about our health insurance package for the coming year. I had put off this visit for as long as possible, but the day had come in which I needed to make a decision. The following questions kept going through my mind as I awaited the visit from the agent. Would the office visit co-payment increase again for staff? What about prescriptions—would generics still be at a discount? What percentage of the insurance premium would the organization be able to afford toward each staff member's policy? Would we be able to afford anything toward spousal or dependent coverage?

I knew the message from the agent would be very similar to the messages from past years: increased costs for the same or lesser medical benefits for our staff. In fact, during my time as the leader of this particular nonprofit human service organization, I witnessed health insurance rates for our employees increase by an average of 20 percent on an annual basis, with some quotes from certain insurance carriers rising as high as 30 percent over the prior year's premium—most often for less elaborate benefits than the prior year. Thus, I routinely had to make a choice between absorbing increased costs and passing the increases on to our employees in the form of a higher percentage contribution toward the insurance premium.

The health insurance premium expense was what our organization needed to pay in order to provide group health coverage for the employees. Health insurance coverage was one of the elements of the *total compensation* (this will be explained later in this chapter) package at our organization. We had choices as to how to handle the insurance benefit for our employees: the insurance premium expense could be fully paid by the organization (not very feasible for my organization or any organization, frankly) or shared with employees also making contributions toward their insurance premiums. Sure, I could have passed the increased premium cost along to the employees in the form of a higher employee contribution for that particular year, but how appropriate would that have been given that many of our employees were not earning very high salaries, not to mention that some were self-identified mental health consumers with already high out-of-pocket expenses for certain psychotropic medications and for psychotherapy visits beyond what were covered by the insurance plan?

Attempting to balance the financial and the human resource demands of the organization, I worked with my finance staff to analyze the overall agency budget to eliminate some other less necessary expenses in order to absorb much of the health insurance rate hike, therefore not passing on the increased expense to our employees. Cutting costs and establishing expense priorities within a human service agency is challenging, but it is often necessary in order to ensure that the talent of the organization, in this case the employees, is cared for in the best way possible. Chapter 7 will touch on the topic of health insurance expenses a bit more from a broader policy standpoint and explain how providing health insurance coverage is an ongoing, if not the foremost, challenge for the management of today's human service organizations. The key point for now is that your talent—your valued staff members, board members, and volunteers—are essential to the effective delivery of social work services. Simply put, if you do not take care of your talent as best as you can, which often involves prudent financial management and the balancing of financial concerns with human concerns, service delivery could ultimately suffer. Essentially, had I passed on the increased cost of health insurance to staff members, our services may have been negatively affected due to employee dissatisfaction, low morale, employee turnover, and so forth.

Social Work as a Service Business

Throughout all sectors of the economy, there are two main types of businesses: those that sell products and those that sell services. Some of these businesses also produce the products and services that they sell, but not all do. Most, if not all, social work organizations are in the business of selling (more on this process in Chapter 4), and often producing, various social services to customers, which, in our field, we usually refer to as clients or consumers.

Service businesses are unique from product businesses in a couple of key ways. First, the nature of the relationship between customer and service provider, or client and social worker, is essential to the success of the social service being offered. Second, the way feedback from customers is used in decision-making is highly important. In many social work program settings, but admittedly not all, client feedback gets incorporated into the service delivery mechanism. Essentially, effective service businesses typically have a customer orientation or mindset, in that all organizational efforts are ultimately focused on satisfying the customer's needs (Andreasen & Kotler, 2003). In social work organizations, our primary customers most often are our clients, the beneficiaries of the human services provided by an organization. Thus, social work is a prime example of a service business and this mindset should pervade all that social workers and social work managers do.

The Relationship between Customer and Service Provider

The first unique characteristic of a service business as opposed to a product business is that the nature of the relationship between the customer and the service provider is highly important to service delivery. First and foremost, nearly all services are delivered by people, and a customer's experience with a service is dependent upon his or her interactions with the person providing that particular service. This relationship contrasts with that occurring in a product business. When companies sell products, there is often little to no relationship between the entity (e.g. a supermarket) selling the product and the end customer. Obviously, many product retailers make efforts to connect with customers in novel ways. In fact, in some industries, such as the auto industry, salespeople make many efforts to build relationships with prospective and continuing customers. Still, I would argue that many of these relationships are superficial at best. When is the last time you purchased a product because of the relationship you have with a particular seller? Chances are there were many other qualities of the product, such as the price, that motivated you to buy it.

In contrast, social work is inherently a service business. In social work organizations, we need staff to comprehensively understand the customers (clients) and, therefore, we must ensure that staff members are given the necessary tools and resources to do so. For these reasons, Nayar (2010) argues that a service-related organization should pay close attention to its talent and employ an *employee first* mentality rather than only focusing on customers, which is the more traditional *customer first* mentality.

Bank tellers, real estate agents, food servers, teachers, and so forth all provide services to people. In the same way, social workers provide services to the public, the quality of which are ultimately judged by the ability of the social worker to understand where the customer or client is coming from and to form positive relationships. Unlike purchasing a car, as described above, a prospective social work client may in fact choose to attend a particular program (or choose to maintain his or her attendance) based almost entirely on a positive relationship formed with the social worker. Importantly, clients in social work programs can be easily deterred from participating due to negative relations with staff members, thus social work managers must closely monitor the nature of the relationships between staff and clients.

When social workers or other staff in a human service program or organization are managed in a dignifying manner by the leaders of their organizations and provided with the necessary training and development to succeed, they are able to more readily and eagerly form meaningful relationships with the organization's clients, the customers that must always be the centerpiece of a social worker's work. Put simply, people generally treat others the way they are treated themselves. When a social work manager treats staff members with respect and dignity, this often translates into staff relating to clients with similar respect and dignity.

Furthermore, services, unlike products, are often intangible. For instance, we cannot hold a counseling session in our hands and marvel at its features in the same way we can with an iPhone. This makes the relationship between the customer and the service provider even more important in social work—it is often the only tangible part of the service delivery process. If a customer cannot easily see the service, the provider must be able to effectively communicate the service's worth or value. Leadership in social work organizations can model this behavior by seeking to effectively communicate and explain the various programs within organizations. It is not usually obvious to social workers how services are structured and why programs exist. Hence, social work managers can help staff members better connect with clients by providing ongoing training, development, and clear communication.

Using Feedback from Customers in Decision-Making

The second unique aspect of service businesses as opposed to product businesses is the way that customer feedback must continually be used to shape service delivery. It is often difficult at first to judge customer sentiment toward a service, especially toward social work services. When Apple releases a new iPhone, for example, we can judge the popularity of this product by seeing people using the phone on the street or by simply tracking the sales of the new phone over a certain period of time. By comparison, how do we know whether a new supportive housing service, for instance, is popular with formerly homeless clients? The immediate feedback mechanism is not always clear for a social work service such as this.

Still, social work managers are able to judge the popularity or the demand of human services by quite simply asking clients on a routine basis about the services that are being delivered and whether they have any suggestions for improvement of these services. There are a variety of evaluation techniques that social work managers may employ, such as client satisfaction surveys, suggestion boxes, focus groups with clients, and so forth. The key is not what method is used, but rather whether a social work program does anything to incorporate feedback from clients to inform the future provision of services. Too often, social work programs neglect to spend sufficient energy on collecting and analyzing client feedback, which is essential for a service business to be successful.

Moreover, social workers in human service organizations may feel that their service delivery work is ineffective and not impacting people. Consequently, their motivation to do the work may decrease. This is another reason why utilizing customer feedback is so important to service businesses. Without such information, there is really no way to understand how services can be enhanced for greater satisfaction, or how those delivering services can know that what they are doing is making any difference.

Managing Downward

As mentioned in the introduction to this chapter, in the for-profit sector many companies like to refer to their employees as talent, which implies that there is an inherent positive value to the people that create the company's products or carry out the services of the company (Conaty & Charan, 2010). In contrast, in the human service arena, referring to staff members or employees as talent is not too common. More often, talent management in the human services, often referred to as the management of human resources or as personnel management, is transactional in nature. Activities are often focused around how to write a job description, post a job advertisement, interview, hire, discipline, terminate, and so forth. These are the day-to-day transactions that frequently pass as talent management in the human services. Although all of these transactions are necessary and should be learned by social work managers and students, little time and energy is spent on nurturing the talents of people already working for the human service organization and developing future talent for new positions. A focus on talent as opposed to transactions, I argue, will benefit any human service organization. The following are some ways in which talent management may manifest itself in a human service organization.

Developing the Talent Pipeline

One of the most important, and often the most elusive, aspects of talent management is ensuring that there is a sufficient pipeline, or supply, of capable individuals to fill positions at your organization. This is not something that should be taken for granted in today's human service industry. Over the past decade, anxiety has grown over whether human service organizations can meet the growing demand for leadership and other key talent brought by overall sector growth and an approaching boom in executive-level retirements (Solomon & Sandahl, 2007; Tierney, 2006; Bell, Moyers, & Wolfred, 2006; Forbes Funds, 2004). At the same time, the human service sector is rebounding, as evidenced by post-recession job growth in nonprofit organizations generally speaking (Frazier, 2011). Therefore, there is often very little time to begin seeking talent for jobs in your program or organization *after* the jobs become available. It is much better to have a pipeline of suitable talent ready to fill these jobs so that you can move quickly to continue services or start new ones.

So, what can be done to develop the talent pipeline? One relatively simple way is to establish social work internship opportunities within your program or organization and partner with a local college or university's school of social work to provide field placement interns to your organization. If you completed your undergraduate or graduate social work degree program, you should understand very well the value that student interns bring to a program or organization. Social work interns not only receive field instruction and academic credit toward their social work degrees, but also you are spending time training them and acculturating them to your program or organization while they serve as interns. In this way, you are developing the talent pipeline of your program or organization. After the internship, these individuals could be excellent choices to fill positions at your program or organization. Sure, you may be thinking that this is such an obvious recommendation since, if you are reading this book, you may already be serving as a social work intern at an agency that has an internship program in place. Still, I challenge you to think about whether this internship program is viewed as a talent pipeline or simply as a means to get necessary work done at the agency. I would surmise that the latter is most often the case at human service organizations; little time is spent thinking about social work internships as pathways to actual jobs at the organization. This is precisely the way that many MBA internships are conceptualized in contrast, and it is quite common for graduates of MBA programs to land jobs at companies for which they previously served as interns. Social work can follow this same model.

The talent pipeline for your program or organization may also be developed by having a consistent presence in the community. I am not talking about simply going to outreach meetings or program-related events. While these are necessary activities and can help to influence the talent pipeline, what really needs to happen is for the program or organization to expand its reach into parts of the community that are less familiar. If you operate in an urban setting, for example, you could set up a table for your program or organization at a street fair. Spend time talking with people about what you do. There may not be a particular purpose for these conversations or available jobs to discuss, but you are meeting people who could potentially become employees. These people can also spread the word about your work to their connections, thereby enhancing the profile of your program or organization in the broader community.

Making Optimal Hiring Decisions

After issues of talent pipeline development have been addressed and there are available positions at your organization, the next step is to decide how to make the smartest hiring decisions. It is rather difficult in nonprofit organizations—and often much more difficult in public-sector agencies—to remove staff if a bad hire was made. Therefore, it is essential to make the best hiring decision possible to avoid future staffing problems.

I recommend involving as many people from your program or organization as feasible in the hiring process without bogging down the process too much. At the university where I work, it is customary to form hiring committees for nearly all new hires. I applaud the use of committees for many reasons. Perhaps most importantly, a committee allows for more than one person to interview, evaluate, and share feedback about job candidates. On the other hand, a downside of hiring committees can be that it is cumbersome to organize schedules and move through the hiring process in a nimble manner. You will need to find a balance between involving multiple parties and still being efficient in the hiring process.

Structuring the Workforce

Despite claims that you may hear about certain organizations with very progressive cultures (e.g. social media companies such as Facebook) that may not have standard organizational structures in place, it is important in human service organizations to organize the workforce appropriately based on the types of services offered and the scope of the organization. Actually, most companies of a certain size, regardless of industry, have a set structure in place. The structure of an organization or program is commonly illustrated by an organizational chart (in some professional circles, this is called a table of organization). Organizational charts can be rather easily designed by using Microsoft PowerPoint, which is how I designed the sample organizational charts shown in Figures 3.1 and 3.2.

An example of an organization with a functional structure is depicted in Figure 3.1. In this type of organization, each function, such as human resources, information technology, and the various programs, is represented by its own branch on the organizational chart. Each branch of the organization performs a specific function. For example, the human resources department provides support to all of the other areas of the organization, regardless of where these areas fall on the organizational

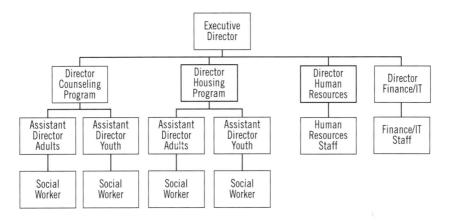

Figure 3.1 Organizational Chart—Functional Structure

chart. Functional structures are probably the most common in the human service industry, especially in the nonprofit sector.

In contrast, an organization with a divisional structure differs from one with a functional structure, in that each division, or branch of the organizational chart, is responsible for all of its functional processes within the division. It is often easiest to think of divisional structures as collections of mini-organizations within a larger whole: each mini-organization is self-contained for the most part and can perform its functions within its division. Figure 3.2 depicts an organization that follows a divisional structure. In this example, the adult division contains all of the necessary functions needed to run the division: human resources, finance, information technology, and the various programs. In this type of organization, there is often little crossover between divisions, which lends itself well to very large organizations that might be split up by geography, for instance. A national human service nonprofit organization could have East Coast, Midwest, and West Coast divisions, as an example. Many government departments also follow a divisional structure since they are often quite large and need to divide functions into various divisions.

There are still other structures that human organizations may have, including matrix or bottom-up types of structures. In a matrix structure, there are multiple reporting relationships and often employees have more

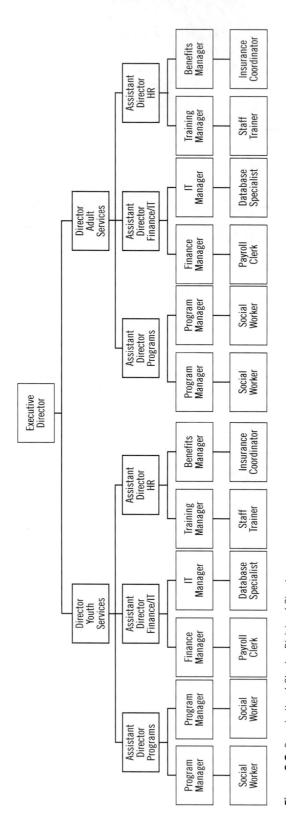

Figure 3.2 Organizational Chart—Divisional Structure

than one supervisor depending on the particular projects that they are working on. Matrix structures are hard to depict and also quite difficult to implement, but the important thing to remember is that they do not follow a strictly hierarchical pattern like divisional or functional structures. Additionally, some social work organizations prefer to flip the organizational chart and include clients at the top of the hierarchy, therefore clients are in theory at the helm of the organization, with all else flowing from there. These alternative structures are not common in the human service arena, but you should know that they exist and be able to interpret them as necessary.

Performance Management and Talent Development

People who work in the human services often receive very little feedback about their work from the people they serve. Thus, human service employees frequently do not know where they stand as far as job performance. The social work manager can help mitigate this information gap by developing and maintaining a system of performance management, which essentially involves communicating regularly with staff members about their job performance.

According to Mathis and Jackson (2011), effective performance measurement must include performance standards that are connected to an employee's job description. Often, performance is measured by an instrument called a performance appraisal, which is essentially a list of items for which an employee is responsible accompanied by an area for written comments related to each item. Ideally, the performance appraisal will include some sort of quantitative scoring system so that the social work manager can rate staff members in each category of performance and compare scores for different employees on each job item and for total performance.

Although the performance appraisal process seems straightforward, Weinbach and Taylor (2011) describe a common situation that occurs within social work organizations in which neither the social work manager nor the social worker he or she supervises is comfortable with the performance evaluation and management process. To mitigate such discomfort, the social work manager should schedule to meet regularly with each supervisee to discuss job performance. These meetings ideally would occur at a minimum every three months; they should ideally be more frequent, even weekly, if program conditions allow.

In addition to performance management and other administrative aspects of talent management and supervision, Kadushin and Harkness (2002) also stress the importance of educational and supportive supervision in a social work environment. Educational components of talent management include helping employees learn to do their jobs better. Training and professional development are popular ways to do this and important to enhancing and maintaining the overall productivity of your staff members. As Brody (2005) suggests, the best training occurs while the work is being performed and, therefore, social work managers can often find ways to support such on-the-job training without having to spend large amounts from otherwise constrained budgets. Finally, supportive supervision involves helping social workers cope with the stressful aspects of their jobs, which are unfortunately almost always part of the work in the human service industry. Social work managers can again meet regularly with employees to listen and provide support, as well as partner with employee assistance programs to refer certain employees for more intensive support services should this level of support become necessary. Employee assistance programs are surprisingly economical for organizations to adopt. Typically, you can add an employee assistance benefit for your employees by way of your health and life insurance package. Your insurance agent can inform you about options for offering an employee assistance program, a very worthwhile investment in your organization's talent.

Taking Care of Your People: The Total Compensation View

As illustrated in Table 3.1, the concept of total compensation involves a variety of elements included in an employee's compensation package that go beyond merely cash compensation. Messmer and Bogardus (2008) describe this view as encompassing direct and indirect compensation, which together can be used to attract and retain talent. For example, in Table 3.1, the category of money illustrates direct compensation elements, which include various cash payments made to employees. The other compensation categories in Table 3.1 represent indirect components of total compensation. Offering child care services

TALENT MANAGEMENT

Table 3.1 Elements of Total Compensation

Compensation Category	Examples of Compensation Types
Money	• salary • cash bonuses • overtime pay • deferred retirement pay
Insurance	• medical • dental • life • disability • professional liability • discounts on automobile and homeowner
Time Benefits	• vacation • sick • flextime • bereavement • special day (e.g. birthday) • compensatory • volunteering
Professional Development	• paid training and continuing education • tuition remission • conference attendance and travel • subscriptions to professional publications
Other	• child care • agency vehicle use • health club memberships • discounts on movie tickets, restaurants, etc.

to employees, for instance, is not a direct cash payment, but rather a benefit that will most likely be very helpful to many employees and one that these employees would view as a valuable and attractive aspect of total compensation.

Managing Upward

It may sound counterintuitive at first, but in addition to taking care of your team and managing the talent within your program or organization, successful social work managers also must manage their superiors. I refer to this process as managing upward. Yes, managing your boss, or, at times, several bosses, will help you to succeed as a social work manager. But how does this work? The following are a few examples of how and where a social work manager can manage upward depending on where one sits within an organization.

Board Relations and Board Development

Typically, a human service organization is governed by a board of directors, a group of volunteers that agree to oversee the operations and integrity of the organization. Brothers and Sherman (2012) describe the role of the board as highly important to nonprofit organizations, but with a duty that is challenging to execute because, at least in the case of nonprofits, we expect volunteer boards of directors to function effectively even though members have little to no training or knowledge of corporate governance. Notice that the board of directors is not a part of the organizational chart in either Figure 3.1 or Figure 3.2. This is because the board in almost all human service organizations is not part of the paid staff of an organization, but rather is a body of volunteers that oversee the work of the organization. Still, boards are ultimately responsible for everything that occurs in a human service organization. If this sounds like a lot of duty to bear for the board members, it certainly is. Moreover, board members, being volunteers, may not have a background in human service organizations or be provided with routine training similar to what might be offered to the management staff. It is the job of the chief executive of the organization (e.g. the CEO or executive director) to manage the volunteer board of directors while, at the same time, it is the duty of the board of directors to manage the chief executive. In essence, this is both an upward and downward management scheme. This is an interesting dynamic that is somewhat unique to nonprofit organizations. Below in the "Perspectives from the Field" section is an interview with a nonprofit human service CEO that should shed some light on the relationship between a chief executive and a board of directors in a human service organization, and how an executive can manage upward in this situation.

TALENT MANAGEMENT

Succession Planning

What happens to human service organizations when a key leader or staff member retires, resigns, or is terminated from employment? What about a changeover in the leadership of the board of directors, such as a chairperson resigning from duty or moving out of the geographical area? When these events occur, is there a plan in place to continue the delivery of services and the seamless leadership of the organization despite the changes in talent? Such a plan of action is known as a succession plan and should be in place for any program or organization. By their very nature, succession plans are a method of managing upward since these plans are created for those higher up in an organization to understand what to do in the event of a departure of a key staff member.

There are basically two types of succession plans that human service organizations can develop: a non-emergency and an emergency succession plan. A non-emergency succession plan will outline what should happen in the event of a planned departure of a key staff member, manager, or leader from the organization. This type of plan will most likely include sufficient time to recruit and train new talent to replace the departing talent. In contrast, an emergency succession plan is one that accounts for the necessary actions of an organization when a key member of the team suddenly departs without warning. Emergency succession plans often include instructions or a checklist for who should cover which aspects of the key person's job immediately after the key person has departed from the organization. The emphasis in an emergency plan is in quickly lining up people to ensure that service delivery is uninterrupted; recruiting and developing new talent is of secondary importance in an emergency succession plan.

Supervisor Relations

Whether your supervisor works alongside you in the same program, or is at another physical location within your organization, your relationship with this supervisor is one that needs to be cultivated. If you happen to be a first-line social work supervisor or manager in which you are directly responsible for service provision to clients, you are most likely far removed from the top management of your organization. However, your supervisor is one step closer to this important group of agency leaders.

As a new social work manager or a student in a field placement, it may seem unimportant to develop strong relationships with your supervisor or with senior leaders at your organization via your supervisor. However, one reason to do so is that almost all organizational policies are developed at the senior levels of human service organizations. You will be able to have your voice (and the voice of your clients) heard more frequently and effectively if you have a solid relationship with your supervisor. In addition, when it comes time for promotions to higher positions in the organization, having good relationships with those higher up the chain of command can help you to be considered for these promotional opportunities. I was once invited to interview for an executive director position at an agency where I worked based on relationships I had cultivated with senior leadership. I ended up not being chosen for the position, but it was my practice of managing upward that allowed me to even be considered for the role.

Adding Value through Stretch Assignments

While social workers and other professionals can quite easily carry out their careers by strictly following the duties described in their job descriptions, it is the social worker that takes on new assignments outside of his or her job duties—*stretch assignments*—that is viewed as a prime candidate for promotional opportunity at the organization. Further, taking on new assignments can also help to prepare you for seeking an advancement opportunity at a different organization. While this scenario will not directly benefit your present employer, you should view stretch assignments as a way to enhance your skill set for more effective management practice and for future promotional opportunities. There is a common saying in business: "Work toward the job you want, not the job you have." This means that you should envision having a higher-level job as you go about your daily routine. This mindset should allow you to add value in your current role, therefore managing upward by making your supervisor pleased, while also positioning yourself appropriately for the next highest level when the opportunity arises to take on the new challenge.

Perspectives from the Field: Working with a Board of Directors

The following are excerpts of an interview I conducted with Cassandra Loch LCSW, MBA, president and CEO of Prototypes, Inc. (for more information, visit: www.prototypes.org), a comprehensive community behavioral health organization located in Los Angeles, CA. Cassandra has served as president and CEO of Prototypes since 2008. She has extensive management and leadership experience in both the nonprofit and for-profit sectors in the arena of behavioral healthcare. She holds both MSW and MBA degrees and is a fellow board member of the Network for Social Work Management. I asked Cassandra several questions related to how she *manages up* with her board of directors to whom she directly reports. I anticipate that her perspective will help to highlight some of the themes from this chapter.

In general, what is your relationship like with your board of directors?
My relationships are extremely positive overall with all of our board members. It is true that the board functions at a higher level and we are more connected when we are all in person at meetings. There is certain chemistry at our quarterly board meetings that is harder to maintain between meetings, but it is my job to work to maintain these relationships even when we are not meeting together. With exception of one person on our board, all of the current board members have been introduced to the board by me since I started as president and CEO. There is only one board member still on the board since the founding of the organization, which was before I joined. This member is indeed emotionally tied to the organization's founders, which can sometimes be a challenging situation to navigate, but others don't have such ties because I introduced them to the board.

What does a typical day look like with regard to board relations?
Leading up to our quarterly board meetings is pretty intense. I try to prepare board members in advance of these meetings by providing board information packets a week before each meeting. Still, I find that not all board members read this information in advance. I think many of them trust me and the rest of the

management team so much that they don't read everything in detail. I also spend a lot of time on event planning with board members and with the fundraising committee of the board. When planning an event, several times a week I talk with members involved in these activities. In addition, we have an audit committee and investment committee that each meets a couple of times a year. We also have a succession planning committee, which is new, to plan for the future. I am a member of all of these committees and need to ensure that the committee work—and other necessary work of the board—continues even between formal board meetings. We also have a support group called the Prototypes Partners. They plan events and raise awareness for us. I meet with them monthly to quarterly.

How do your relationships vary among your various board members? This is an issue and you need to figure out what the various styles are and what is interesting to them as far as the organization is concerned. We are trying to bring younger generations onto the board to diversify our members and also plan for eventual succession. A whole new and different dynamic evolves when younger people come to the board. We are also talking about developing a junior board with younger people that can eventually succeed board members when they resign or retire. Still, our more experienced board members are highly important to us. For example, one person on the board that has been around the longest is also an employment law attorney and helps out the agency on pro bono basis. In addition, she offers a wonderful historical perspective for newer board members.

What is your strategy for developing the talent of your board? We have eight board members total. When I came to the organization seven years ago, the former CEO was still there. The board we had at that time had been in place since the agency's founding. I brought in an expert board development consultant, someone external to teach our board about their roles. They had social work and program expertise and were friends with the founders but they were not experts on governance principles. A few board members self-selected out at that time because they were thinking of leaving the board anyway once they knew that things were going to work out with me. For some, they felt that the new board culture was not for them. I slowly brought in professional connections from other settings. We needed people at that point and not so much their specific skill sets. After that point, in the second phase of board development, we started actively recruiting people. In this phase, we developed a grid of skill sets that were wanted on the board: financial, legal, etc. We mapped out who was on the board and where the holes in talent were. We also wanted people that would be passionate about what Prototypes does. Mental health consumers with personal experience were also important to consider. Our bylaws allow for 15 board members total. I try to add two or three new people per year as some members rotate off the board. Many of our board members are overextended so the amount of time they can dedicate is limited. At this point in time, I think we may need a different level of expertise. We are starting to evolve into our next phase of board recruitment—we are looking for people to shake things up a little and help us become a fundraising board.

In your opinion, what is the purpose of a nonprofit board?
I struggled with this at first as an executive. My gut reaction is fundraising—the board should bring in revenue and help sustain the organization in a meaningful way. Obviously governance and fiduciary duties are essential from a technical standpoint. Our board members have an amazing amount of trust in me and others that work here. I think it's hard to be a nonprofit board member. You are not there every day. Trust is important with the staff. Corporate board members get paid and often the information they get is greater, especially when companies are publicly traded. I think that some people might initially join a nonprofit board as a resume builder, for networking, or because it is good for their business. Fortunately, all of our board members are passionate about our organization's work. Most

think their job is to spread the word about the agency and not so much the actual governance—this is an interesting phenomenon with a nonprofit board. And it can be a healthy tension between management and the board.

How is reporting to a board different from other reporting relationships that social work managers may encounter?
There are far fewer day-to-day interactions in my experience. The entire process of reporting and managing upward becomes so critical more than any other role. Unless something bad ends up in the paper, no one from the board will call you. You are solely responsible for getting them the information. What is important for them to know? What do they need to know? Day-to-day management is not their role. If you are moving from a middle management to an executive position, you need a complete shift in thinking because you are not reporting everything to a board. Don't come to the board with little stuff. Bring solutions, not just problems, to the board members.

How did you develop such a "filtering" system?
It was interesting. The board I inherited didn't want to know anything really. I found that I was over-communicating in a purposeful way so they could get more involved. I then learned to adjust and give them the right balance of information. It really depends on the context. The danger for someone who is new to an executive position is not being able to find that balance of communication and information flow. You don't want to over-communicate but you also don't want to under-communicate with the board of directors.

What suggestions do you have for social work managers regarding working with boards? How can emerging leaders get the attention of board members?
There's a lot you can do in this area. You could volunteer yourself on a nonprofit board, junior board, or development committee. Find a place where there is some sophistication to learn how this whole process works. If you are willing to volunteer on a

TALENT MANAGEMENT

committee or plan an event, you would get exposure to other people because boards are involved in these sorts of things. In most major cities, finding those classes that nonprofits put on that talk about skills you need to become an executive director might also be helpful. You don't want to annoy or create more work for board members at your organization, but somehow you want to gain board relations skills if you aspire to move up to the executive level in a nonprofit human service organization.

What should social work students know about boards—what do you wish you had learned in your MSW program?
Being politically savvy is the most important thing. Is it possible to teach that and, if so, how would it be taught? I am not sure. You don't always know it when you see it but you sure know when someone is or when you are not politically savvy. To master this, you really need someone who is not an academic, perhaps a mentor who is a practitioner to talk with you about what you need to know. This doesn't come from a theoretical place at all in my opinion.

Managing Sideways

Thus far, this chapter has explored methods for effectively managing your talent or team (managing downward), as well as strategies for successfully managing upward with a board of directors or other superiors at your organization. I argue that it is also an essential skill in the realm of talent management to be able to *manage sideways* in an organized and strategic manner. Managing sideways involves engaging with those in your professional network that are not formally connected to you on the organizational chart. This may include people both inside and outside of your organization. Think of your professional network as a complex web of connections. There are some obvious connections downward, such as your supervisees and others that you may manage. Additionally, there are often clear connections upward—your boss, for example. But what about those lateral connections in your professional network? What about mentors, either formal or informal, with which you have an ongoing relationship? What about your fellow classmates in your social work program (or fellow alumni if you have already graduated)? These are people that do no report directly to you or to whom you report, but these people can be very helpful to you as a practicing social work manager. You can also add value to them as a part of their sideways or lateral network.

Developing Strategic Networks

Watkins (2003) describes coalition building with people in your professional network as an important step in gaining legitimacy for any new manager or leader in the corporate world. I posit that the same holds true for any social work manager regardless of the level of position within a social work program or organization. The more embedded you can situate yourself within your professional network—both inside and outside of your organization—the easier it will be to accomplish your objectives.

It is also important to build strategic partnerships and networks with other organizations. These types of arrangements can be mutually beneficial to both your organization and to your partnering organization. A good example of strategic network building in the human services is joining trade associations or advocacy coalitions. In almost all areas of the human services, there exist such organizations, and you should become an active member if possible. Your local chapter of the National Association of Social Workers (NASW) is another good example of an organization available for strategic partnering. Such partnerships will not only benefit you professionally, but also other staff members and often the clients in your program or organization.

Internal versus External Connections

There are important networks both within and outside of any social work manager's organization. Typically, we think that connections within our organization are the most helpful. Managers of other programs, for example, can often be sought after for general management advice or to provide coverage to your program should you need to be absent for whatever reason. Additionally, certain staff members, such as assistants to senior leaders or executives, could be useful connections to you when you need to get answers to particular questions and do not have access to the leadership of your organization. These types of people are often called gatekeepers because they allow you access to higher levels of the organization. These are a few examples of why it might be worthwhile to build internal connections at your organization.

Increasingly, external connections—people outside of the organization where you work or do your field placement—are becoming important for social work managers. A social work manager with an array of external connections can call upon many experts, for instance, to troubleshoot various issues at a program or organization. As such, this social work manager adds a great deal of value to his or her program or organization because of the external connections that can be leveraged. The more you can leverage such connections, the more value you can add to your current work.

Social Networking as a Talent Management Tool

Social networking has been on the rise for several years both in a personal sense and for organizational uses. Chapter 7 will provide more specifics on social networking and media uses in human service organization. But for talent management purposes, it is sufficient to know that these tools are now essential to managing and leveraging both internal and external connections. A particularly useful tool for keeping tabs on your professional network is LinkedIn, a social media site that is designed for professional purposes. Every social work manager or student should develop a LinkedIn profile and begin to leverage it—your ability to manage sideways will be greatly enhanced by using a tool such as LinkedIn.

Chapter Summary

This chapter began with an introduction to the concept of talent management in a human service organization as opposed to a more traditional personnel management paradigm. After a practice example related to balancing financial and talent management, I explained how social work should be viewed as a service business similar to other types of service businesses that exist in the for-profit realm. Then, the chapter explored ways in which social work managers can manage talent in all directions: downward, upward, and sideways. An interview with a nonprofit human services executive was also included to illuminate points made in the chapter.

Some important concepts from this chapter to be sure to understand are as follows:

- The human resources or personnel of a social work organization should be viewed as talent and the process of managing these resources should be referred to as talent management.
- Talent management and financial management must be balanced in social work organizations due to frequently constrained resources and trade-offs that social work managers must make.
- Social work is truly a service business in which the relationship between client and social worker is a key driver of a program's success.
- Effective talent management involves a social work manager knowing how to manage in all directions: downward, upward, and sideways.

Suggested Learning Exercises

- Create an organizational chart of the program or agency where you work or have your field placement. (*Hint*: you can use Microsoft PowerPoint to design the chart. Start with one of the templates and modify as necessary.) Examine the formal structure of the program or agency and make note of any informal links between employees not captured on the chart. What type of structure is your program or agency—functional, divisional, or some other type? How might you include clients and volunteers in your chart? How can you enhance this program or organizational structure to allow for more effective operations? How might you manage sideways given this organizational structure?
- With a partner that works at or has a field placement at an organization different from yours, compare and contrast the *total compensation* offerings of both organizations. In addition to salary, what other benefits are offered to employees at each organization? How attractive do you think each of these total compensation packages is to prospective employees and why? How could you

enhance the total compensation package at your organizations without greatly increasing direct expenses? You may want to consult the websites of the organizations and the human resource offices for details on what is offered.

- Make a list of at least three stretch assignments that would allow you to develop your strategic network for career growth. For each stretch assignment, discuss how it will enhance your skill set and also how it will add value to your current program or organization (if you are not presently working, think about this in relation to your fieldwork placement). With a classmate, pretend that you are meeting with your supervisor to discuss your desire to take on stretch assignments. Practice what you would say and how you would say it.

- Create a LinkedIn profile and add at least five new connections per day for one week. For each new connection request, write a personalized e-mail to the individual requesting a connection. In addition, join at least two groups during the week and post two news articles or comments in each of these groups. Finally, "like" at least five items over the course of the week. Discuss your performance for the week—number of total connections, number of "likes" on your updates, etc.—with a classmate. Discuss how you could enhance your LinkedIn strategy to build a more expansive professional network. If you are really ambitious, repeat this exercise for a number of weeks to see how your LinkedIn network develops. Do not forget to connect with your classmates —and your professor! Connect with me, too, if you would like!

Internet Resources

Society for Human Resource Management—the world's largest organization dedicated to the management of talent and human resources. The website contains a wealth of information and articles on nearly all aspects of talent and human resource management: www.shrm.org.

Idealist—one of the most popular websites for job posting and talent seeking in the nonprofit sector. The site also contains an active community of bloggers and a variety of other helpful resources related to managing a nonprofit organization's talent: www.idealist.org.

BoardSource—an organization that helps develop the capacity of non-profit boards of directors and executive management teams. Much of BoardSource's offerings are fee-based, but there is also some useful information available for free on its website: www.boardsource.org.

Bridgestar—an initiative of the Bridgespan Group, a popular nonprofit sector consultancy, offering articles and tools related to talent acquisition, management, and retention in the nonprofit sector. The website also features a comprehensive job board for open management, board member, and executive positions: www.bridgespan.org/About/Bridgestar. aspx.

LinkedIn—an essential social media tool for building your strategic professional network. All social work management students and professionals should maintain an active LinkedIn profile—it is free and easy to set up: www.linkedin.com.

GuideStar—a clearinghouse of information related to the U.S. nonprofit sector, including downloadable Internal Revenue Service Form 990s and various free articles related to managing people and other aspects of nonprofit management. Create an account for free to view and download content: www.guidestar.org.

Teampedia.net—a collaborative Web-based encyclopedia based on the popular Wikipedia model in which users can post and read about icebreakers, team-building exercises, and other tools for enhancing the productivity of teams in the workplace: www.teampedia.net.

National Staff Development and Training Association—a U.S.-based membership organization dedicated to building professional and organizational capacity in the human service sector through the sharing of ideas and resources related to organizational development, staff development, and training. The organization sponsors an annual conference, publishes a professional journal, and maintains a website with a variety of helpful resources: http://nsdta.aphsa.org/default.htm.

TALENT MANAGEMENT

Succession Planning—the nonprofit consultancy CompassPoint (www. compasspoint.org) publishes on its website a variety of useful tools for succession planning in nonprofit organizations, including succession plan templates and other items available for free download: www.compass point.org/et.

4
MARKETING, SALES, AND COMMUNICATIONS

Once you have sufficiently understood and analyzed your program or organization's finances (themes from Chapter 2), and you are able to successfully understand and manage your program or organization's talent (topics of Chapter 3), it is time to focus on the processes of marketing, sales, and communications. At a high level, these processes involve understanding the market demand for your services, publicizing the current work you are doing at your program or organization, and beginning to develop new business opportunities. One reason for publicizing your current work in a nonprofit human service organization, for instance, might be to increase awareness of your programs in an effort to raise more funds for the organization. Prospective funders typically want to understand what programs an organization is undertaking and what results have been obtained before committing funding to an organization.

Public or for-profit human service organizations need to also publicize their work and develop new business even if they are not engaged in the traditional fundraising process. Still, these types of organizations could similarly be seeking grants or attempting to disseminate best practices (public sector), or appealing to investors or strategic partners (for-profits). Whatever the specific reasons might be for engaging in marketing, sales, and communications activities, all human service organizations need to understand the marketing frameworks for their human services, how to sell and develop new customers or clients, and how to communicate both internally and externally regarding the work of the organization.

This chapter will begin with an overview of the marketing process as it pertains to human service organizations, including a discussion of the common marketing frameworks used to effectively market human services. I will then introduce the concept of sales and discuss the importance of selling ideas both inside and outside of a human service organization. The chapter will conclude with a section on useful communications tactics that can be implemented by social work managers in the management of a human service program or organization.

Marketing Is More Than Just Advertising

I have heard social work managers say many times, "We must market this new service to our clients!" But what does this really mean? To me, people usually mean to say *advertising* when they use the word *marketing* in a human service context. Marketing a human service involves far more than simply advertising, or promoting the service to one particular group, in this case prospective clients of the program. Instead, marketing is a much broader process of developing a comprehensive understanding of the entire marketplace and all its segments, and properly targeting and positioning your human service to optimize its market share (the proportion of potential clients that choose your service over other comparable services available in the marketplace).

Common Marketing Frameworks: Four P's and STP

One of the most basic yet important marketing frameworks is called the *Four P's framework*. The Four P's are defined as: product, price, place, and promotion. It is a simple rubric to remember, but, when conceptualized correctly, contains a substantial amount of important information related to the marketing strategy for your human service program or organization. Table 4.1 lists some important questions to ask with regard to each of the areas in the Four P's framework as you begin the process of marketing a new service, program, or even an entire organization. The following are brief descriptions of each category.

MARKETING, SALES, AND COMMUNICATIONS 81

First, let us discuss *product*. In most instances, human service organizations are in the business of selling services, not products, therefore I will focus on the marketing of services here. Consequently, you will want to remember that the first "P," the product category, in the Four P's framework often refers to services in our field of human services. It is of primary importance to first think about what service is offered in the program where you work or do your field placement. What are the features of this program that make it different from other comparable programs in the marketplace? By answering this question, you are identifying what differentiates your service from others. Differentiation is a positive quality as it allows your program to stand out from competitors in the market for your service. When thinking about this first "P" in the Four P's framework, your focus should be on fully understanding all aspects of the human service (or product in some select cases) that is being offered. Essentially, if you cannot understand your service, it will most likely not be understood by clients, prospective donors, and the like.

Next, *price* is another key ingredient in any successful marketing effort. What amount are you asking clients to pay for the receipt of your service? Many times, services are free of charge for clients of social work programs. However, this does not mean that a price does not exist. Clients may not pay, or may pay a very minimal amount, but there is a price or a cost for delivering this service. While you may not publicize this price to the clients, this will be very useful information for you to communicate to prospective funders for your program or organization. Funders most often want to know exactly what it costs for you to deliver a particular service. Understanding a service's true price will help you to communicate this information when necessary. As you can see, depending on the audience for which your marketing effort is intended (see next section on *targeting*), you will have corresponding price rationales. Essentially, prospective clients may not be willing to pay anything, whereas prospective funders may be willing to cover the price of the service.

Further, the *place* or location of a human service program or organization can also affect its success in the marketplace. Some programs are embedded in the communities served by the program while other programs may be located a short distance away from the target community. The important thing about location is not necessarily whether a program is located close to or far from clients, but whether there is a rationale for why it is situated one way or the other. That is, there may be good reason for locating a program slightly away from an urban center, as an example. The rent may be prohibitively high, for instance, for an organization to offer a program in the center of a major city. Therefore, the *place* of the service would be optimal further away from the end customer where the service offered could most likely be richer or more comprehensive because less program expense would be allocated toward rent, leaving more funds available for the service. This is just one example of how to rationalize the location of a service. Product companies think about this in the sense of product placement—where should a product be placed on a store shelf to best lure customers to purchase it? The same logic applies to social work services. How can we best lure clients to a program by its location and what are the attributes of its location that would be most attractive to clients?

Finally, *promotion* is a concept that most of us are more familiar with. In fact, promotion is what most social work managers mean to say when they use the term marketing. Promotion is simply another word for advertising. Importantly, when thinking about promotion in the context of a social work manager utilizing the Four P's framework, think about what steps need to be taken to effectively communicate to prospective clients about a particular service. Promotion should not be haphazard. A detailed promotional plan should be developed to sensibly advertise within the constraints (yes, there are always constraints!) of a particular human service program or organization.

In addition to the Four P's framework for understanding the marketing process, there is the popular and effective *segment-target-position (STP) framework* for effectively navigating the marketing effort. STP should be used in conjunction with the Four P's when you are first embarking on any new marketing initiative. Figure 4.1 illustrates the STP framework and it is also described as follows.

Segment refers to segmentation of the market, or the cutting up of the marketplace into manageable and meaningful groups. These groups, or market segments as they are called, should be as homogenous as

Table 4.1 The Four P's Marketing Framework

The Four P's	*Key Questions to Answer*
Product (service)	• What product or service are you selling? • What are its key differentiating features? • Why should customers choose your product or service over others available in the marketplace? • Would you choose your product or service? Why or why not?
Price	• How much do you charge (if anything) for what you offer? • How much are customers willing to pay for your product or service? Does your price match the willingness to pay? • How does your price compare to your competitors' prices for a similar product or service?
Place	• Where do you offer your product or service? • Through what channels do you communicate about what you have to offer? • What is unique about your product or service's placement over similar ones in the marketplace? • Does your placement match the needs of your target audience?
Promotion	• How do customers know about your product or service? • What types of advertising do you use and why? • What is your plan for promotion? • What are the results of your promotional efforts?

possible so that you can generalize about the characteristics of a particular market segment. For example, you may choose to segment the market for a given service by age groups: 15–17 year olds, 18–21 year olds, 22–29 year olds, and so forth. If age group is somehow related to the service that you offer, this might be a sensible way to segment the market. The idea would be that a certain age segment would behave similarly and, essentially, respond to your service in a similar way. Keep in mind that different services may have different segmentation boundaries that make sense for each service. It is rare that you would segment the market in the exact same way for two distinct services.

MARKETING, SALES, AND COMMUNICATIONS

After you have segmented the market for your service in some meaningful way, the next step is to choose the *target* (or multiple targets in some cases) on which you will focus your marketing efforts. Using the age-related example above, your new service may be most appropriate for the 18–21-year-old target market segment. Therefore, all of your marketing efforts should be geared toward this age group and the other age groups should be left out of your marketing efforts, at least for the time being. Ideally, these other age segments would a good match for, and be picked up by, a service offered by another provider, but you really want to hone in on the market segment that makes the most sense for your particular service offering.

Once a target market segment (or multiple targets in some cases) has been chosen for a given service, you will then want to focus your effort on how to best *position* your service in the marketplace in order to gain the largest share possible of your target market segment. This process is often called gaining market share. In essence, you want your service to be the service of choice for all 18–21 year olds, following the example above. Positioning involves various activities, such as strategic pricing, optimizing the location of the service, promotion and advertising, and so forth. The key thing to remember with positioning is that you must zero in on your chosen target market segment and do everything you can to be in an optimal position in the eyes of those in that segment. A good way to conceptualize positioning is that you want people to think of your particular service when they are in the market for this type of service. You want your service to be top of mind for every prospective customer.[1]

Segment the market by demographic characteristics (age, gender, disability, etc.) or by other means in order to yield manageable and relatively homogenous groups.

Target which of these groups (the less segments, the better) your organization or program wishes to approach in order to sell your product or service.

Position the organization or program for success with the target(s) you chose by streamlining all promotional efforts and messaging. The goal is for your target(s) to think of your organization first when seeking a product or service that you offer.

Figure 4.1 The Segment-Target-Position (STP) Marketing Framework

MARKETING, SALES, AND COMMUNICATIONS 85

Conducting Market Research

In conjunction with analyzing your marketing effort using the Four P's and STP frameworks, another very important step in any marketing effort is to conduct research on the segments you intend to target. In fact, most for-profit companies have entire departments devoted solely to the market research function. Importantly, these are not advertising or promotion departments, but hard-core research groups. Social work organizations are not usually as fortunate as to have full-fledged marketing research departments, but Furman and Gibelman (2013) posit that human service organizations have been forced to adopt, albeit in modest ways, a consumerist approach to providing services in which the demands of the consumer market are extremely influential in the service delivery process. As discussed in Chapter 1, understanding the market demand (not just the need) for a particular human service is highly important to identifying and providing the appropriate supply of this service to the marketplace.

Market research can be conducted much the same way that social workers are accustomed to conducting needs assessments within human service organizations. Typically, a questionnaire is developed and administered to a sample of the target market segment that you have identified from performing your STP analysis. Beyond what is typical of a needs assessment, market research questionnaires ask about the willingness to pay for services, the desired location of a service, what the service should ideally look like, and so forth. Similar data can be obtained through conducting focus groups with a sample of the target market segment. With market research, you are trying to gather as much real data, not just estimates of data, from the marketplace as possible to inform the Four P's and STP frameworks, which will in turn inform the marketing plan that you will need to put together before executing any marketing effort.

Developing a Marketing Plan

A marketing plan is a document that serves as a roadmap for the entire marketing effort or campaign. Marketing plans incorporate all of the information that you have already analyzed by following the Four P's and STP frameworks, and from conducting market research. Marketing

86   MARKETING, SALES, AND COMMUNICATIONS

plans vary in format and length depending on the industry in which a product or service is offered and the overall purpose of the document. For example, it could be more rudimentary if used for internal purposes, but more robust if incorporated as part of a formal presentation to external stakeholders. Levinson (1998) contends, in a rather extreme view, that a marketing plan can be as short as three paragraphs as long as it communicates the most essential element: how will your organization or program *position* itself to be *the first choice* of customers? Still, a stand-alone marketing plan that would suffice on balance for a human service program or organization should be comprised of the elements listed below, and be no more than five or six pages in length, ideally. (*Note*: these guidelines are for a marketing plan that is independent of a business plan document. Chapter 5 will discuss the type of marketing plan that is incorporated as a section in a longer business plan.)

- *Executive summary*—in one page or less, describe the overall purpose of the marketing plan and try to spark the interest of the reader.
- *Marketing goal(s)*—in half a page or less, outline the major goals you seek to achieve by implementing the marketing plan, especially specific milestones you wish to reach and the time frames in which you will achieve these milestones.
- *Product/service description*—in no more than one page, provide a concise description of the product or service that you intend to bring to the marketplace, including an explanation of its distinct features and how it is more effective or a better value than comparable services (this is your competition).
- *Target segment(s)*—in approximately half a page, describe your segment-target-position framework with an emphasis on the specific target market segments within which you will position your service, and the rationale for why these targets were chosen.
- *Pricing strategy*—in half a page or less, describe the price that you have placed on the service and your rationale for setting this particular price. Remember that even if a service is free to clients,

MARKETING, SALES, AND COMMUNICATIONS 87

there is still a price or a cost for the service. Nothing is truly free.

- *Location strategy (place)*—in one page or less, discuss where customers or clients will access your service, why you chose that particular location, and, if possible, include visual descriptions (e.g. maps) to help the reader understand your location strategy.
- *Promotional plan*—in one page or less, outline your specific plan for promoting and advertising your service, including a timeline of when you will implement the various components of the plan, and who will be the responsible party for each of these components.
- *Evaluation process*—in approximately half a page, describe how you will determine whether the marketing plan was effective and met its stated goals.
- *Budget*—using the budget template from Figure 2.2 (Chapter 2) or some other budget spreadsheet that you design, estimate what it will cost to carry out the marketing plan.

Selling Internally

First, selling is not the same as marketing. Indeed, the sales effort is a distinct process from marketing, although they are definitely related. Most for-profit companies have both sales departments and marketing departments, and sometimes they are not even well connected. A simple way to remember the difference is that marketing has much more of a research function than does sales. Before a salesperson, or, in this case, you, as the social work manager, can understand what it is you should be selling, market researchers should have already performed a great deal of work and analysis on why, how, where, when, and to whom you should be selling a particular service. Having both sales and marketing functions is a very tall order for human service organizations, I realize. However, you should know how these functions typically manifest themselves in a for-profit environment. They are distinct and yet both are extremely meaningful for successfully launching products and services.

In social work settings, the sales process basically takes two forms: internal selling and external selling. Internal selling could be referred to as *inside sales*—the extent to which a social work manager is able to convince his or her talent within the organization of new ideas for products and services. Much of a social work manager's time, especially as one goes up the ladder within an organization, is devoted to selling, in one way or another, ideas to co-workers or others that play key roles within our organizations.

Getting Everyone on Board with Your Mission and Ideas

Often the most challenging part of implementing any new idea for a program or project is convincing those inside your organization that your idea is worthwhile and that they should stand behind it despite all of the competing demands present in the workplace. While we do not often have the luxury of a fully developed marketing function in social work organizations, it is thus even more important that the social work manager be able to personally rally people inside the program or organization around the mission in general, or the mission of a particular project that he or she wishes to launch. This rallying stage is critical because often social work managers need to rely on the efforts of many internal staff members or volunteers to execute new business ideas. As such, I have always made a point of holding regular staff meetings within programs and within larger organizations to communicate my new ideas and ask for support, outwardly. Social workers and others that work in human service organizations will be much more willing to stand behind your ideas if you communicate openly and involve them in your thinking. Ask for feedback, too. You may not frequently receive feedback, but people do appreciate being given the chance to give you feedback.

Motivating Your Team to Develop and Execute New Business

Once those internal to your organization have been convinced that a new idea for a program or project is worthwhile, you will need to motivate them to stay the course and help the new idea come to fruition. I have always found that the best way to encourage people to both execute my ideas and to develop new business within a program or organization is to give them the latitude to experiment without fear of failure. If you want to encourage innovation and new idea development at your program or organization, you cannot closely monitor, or micro-manage, your staff members. People in the workplace are often motivated by having the autonomy to explore various ideas and to make their own decisions about their work. Sure, this will at times result in failed projects, but staff members will be more apt to develop successful projects if you allow them to pursue their ideas, at least from time to time.

Promoting Ideas to Current Customers, Organization Staff, and Others

While you are working on getting everyone on board and motivating those within your organization to stand behind your new ideas, you also want to make an effort to initially promote your new ideas to current customers, or clients, that might benefit from the new project, staff that may not be as closely involved, and volunteers and other internal people that should know about the new ideas. In a sense, this type of selling is approaching external sales, which will be discussed in the next section. However, since we are still talking about people involved within the confines of your program or organization, this process will still involve inside sales; you do already have some sort of relationship with these people. With customers or clients, staff from other programs and departments, and anyone else that touches your particular program, you want to be extremely open about your ideas and discuss them in a positive light. Be aware that these people may not be as intimately familiar with your specific program. Therefore, you should make sure to provide extra details and answer questions that people may have about what you are pursuing. The more open and transparent you can be, often the more buy-in you will receive from these internal groups.

Selling Externally

In the sales industry or sales departments of for-profit companies, this type of selling is known as outside sales—how you convince those that know little or nothing about you to buy in to what you have to offer, and to literally buy your service or product. This type of selling contrasts considerably with inside sales described in the last section. With inside sales, you often have the benefit of already having some relationship with the prospective buyer of your product or service, or with those that you are trying to convince that your ideas are worthwhile. To be successful with outside sales, in contrast, experts suggest that you should first build the sales relationship before you can expect people to buy your service or product. Building strong sales relationships while also working to sell a product or service is often referred to as consultative selling, in the sense that you are not only selling a product or service to an individual or group, but you are also along the way consulting with them or helping them with a problem that they may have or questions that might arise. It is important to remember that it is ultimately all about the prospective customer and his or her needs rather than your needs or the demands of your organization.

Prospective Customers

In social work management, most often your prospective customers are those potential clients that may want to partake in the services offered by the human service organization where you work or have your field placement. In essence, this is the most important external constituency that exists for a human service organization. This is ultimately the reason we do the work we do. But, ironically, it seems that the least effort is often spent focusing on the sales relationship with prospective customers or clients. Social workers in human service organizations often perform outreach activities to engage potential clients. While these activities are oftentimes quite meaningful, I challenge you to think about outreach and similar activities as outside sales efforts. Imagine that you are operating in a truly competitive marketplace for the type of services offered by your program or organization. You should strive to develop sales relationships as best you can with prospective clients. In social work practice, much of this type of selling is done by outreach specialists or intake workers in certain programs. If you are in a position of management, consider providing some mentorship or training for these professionals with regard to developing strong sales relationships. While it may at first seem like an odd activity for human service professionals who are not accustomed to thinking like salespeople, it should ultimately benefit your program or organization to have professionals who can not only give outreach seminars or process intake forms, but who can also build meaningful relationships with prospective clients and truly practice consultative sales techniques. Even if such activity is not *billable*, it should provide for return on investment in the future.

The Board of Directors

If you are an executive director or CEO, or in a position to somehow work with your organization's board of directors, you want to make sure that all board members are aware of and, ideally, can endorse an idea for a new program or project. The outside sales process is crucial with the board of directors. As Cassandra Loch discussed in the "Perspectives from the Field" section in Chapter 3, the board is most often detached from the organization and only really connected during scheduled board meetings or when the executive makes an effort to communicate with and engage the board. This type of ongoing engagement with a volunteer board of directors is essentially the process of selling externally—the executive needs to sell the board on not only new ideas, but also must ensure that board members understand the important happenings of the organization. Thus, much of an executive's work with a board of directors is focused on selling externally.

Funders

It may seem obvious, but without convincing prospective funders that an idea for a new program or project is worthwhile, it will not matter how much other internal and external selling you do. Funders are a key component of the external sales strategy because they provide the money with which to operate, and, therefore, must be convinced that your program or project idea is worth their investment. It is a prime responsibility of an executive leader of a human service organization to build sales relationships with prospective funders, but it should also be built into the culture of the entire program or organization such that all staff members at all levels understand the importance of building positive relationships with foundation personnel, donors, investors, and so forth. You never know when and where a prospective funder will appear. Hence, it is good practice to prepare most all of your staff members for selling externally.

Media

Another external body to which social work managers should continually sell their ideas is media outlets. Media outlets have the ability to receive messages from a social work manager and cast the messages out to a very wide audience, thereby greatly enhancing visibility for a social work program or organization. Thus, building strong sales relationships with people working for media outlets can have a lasting impact for a program or organization. I have had the most success with print media and have written a number of letters to the editor and editorial articles for local, national, and international newspapers. Although I am not always able to do so, I try as best as possible to forge a relationship with the editor of the newspaper where I wish to place a letter or an editorial piece. In smaller markets and towns, this is much easier to do. With national and international media, it is often quite difficult to make yourself known to the editors. Either way, it is important for social work managers to engage with media, whether print media or some other format. Table 4.2 presents some samples of my writing in various newspapers, which may give you some ideas for selling your program or organization to various media outlets.

Other Stakeholders

Political figures, associations of nonprofits or government agencies, executives from other organizations in your line of work, and academics at colleges and universities can be key audiences with which the social work manager should sell ideas by maintaining open and frequent communication. I have often liked to be in rooms or audiences where no one is a social worker or where nobody has knowledge of the social work issues that I represent on behalf of my program or organization. I find that in these situations, I am able to develop relationships with people interested in my ideas without having as much competition from similar programs or organizations. As much as possible, I recommend attending meetings and networking events where you are outside of your comfort zone. This will be very difficult to do at first, but with this approach, you will really focus on the outside sales process since people will not have a relationship with you nor have much prior knowledge of your area of work.

Communications Essentials

Throughout this chapter, I have alluded to the role that communication plays in the marketing and sales processes. In fact, there would be no

MARKETING, SALES, AND COMMUNICATIONS   93

Table 4.2 Editorial Writing Examples

Editorial Topic and Placement	Intended Audience and Purpose
• Healthcare reform's employer mandate and its potential impact on nonprofit employers • Letter to the *Wall Street Journal* • http://on.wsj.com/ZTRlhk (Germak, 2013, March 4)	• To reach a broad national audience regarding an issue not widely reported—nonprofits and their constituents will feel effects of increased constraints on resources
• Dignity and respect for corporate employees struggling with addiction and behavioral health conditions • Letter to the *Financial Times* • http://on.ft.com/13NqhB7 (Germak, 2013, May 8)	• To reach a corporate audience with concern over how some companies reportedly treat employees with such conditions, and to advocate for more respect and dignity in the workplace
• Preserving the charitable deduction for nonprofit human service organizations • Op-ed in the *Star-Ledger* • http://bit.ly/16ckavs (Germak, 2013, April 27)	• To respond on a statewide level to the Obama administration's repeated attempts to limit the charitable tax deduction for philanthropic gifts
• Encouragement of collaboration between social work professionals in the U.S. and China • Op-ed in the *Global Times* • http://globaltimes.cn/content/791912.shtml (Germak, 2013, June 27)	• To reach an audience of decision-makers in China responsible for implementing new social programs, and to advocate for American cooperation in these efforts

marketing or sales without communications. It is that important. While dedicating a small section of a chapter of this book to communications is by no means adequate, my intention is to offer a few thoughts on the following communications tactics that should be helpful to you as you carry out your marketing and sales efforts, both within and outside of your program or organization.

The 30-Second Elevator Pitch

The elevator pitch got its name from a scenario in which you imagine yourself riding on an elevator (most likely in a skyscraper) next to an influential person and have approximately 30 seconds to succinctly talk about yourself and your business to this person before the elevator doors open and you both go your separate ways. In the context of social work management, such an elevator pitch is an essential tool regardless of whether you ever ride on an elevator. On almost a daily basis as a social work manager, you encounter people for brief moments where having this sort of pitch handy could be very beneficial.

At a minimum, a 30-second elevator pitch is comprised of a succinct statement of the mission of your program, project, or organization. If your official mission statement takes longer than 30 seconds to recite, you will need to shorten it for the purposes of this exercise! After introducing yourself (do not forget about that) and stating your mission, the elevator pitch should contain some sort of action request for what the person could do to help your cause. This does not necessarily need to be a request for money. In fact, it is difficult to explicitly ask for funding in a 30-second pitch. Instead, you could close your pitch by asking the person for his or her business card, for example, or asking if you could meet with him or her sometime in the near future. You would then follow up with him or her when you return to the office and invite him or her to become more involved with your program or organization, as well as inviting him or her to meet with you. Much of the content of the elevator pitch will depend on the context of your interaction, but at a minimum, you should include your *name and title*, your *mission*, and an *action request*.

The Two-Minute Pitch

The two-minute pitch was introduced in Chapter 1, where I described an invitation I received to speak about my entire organization in approximately 90 seconds at a chamber of commerce networking breakfast. Actually, my pitch that morning was just under two minutes and included everything that the 30-second elevator pitch should include, plus I also had just enough time to include a very brief success story about a client in one of our programs. Therefore, the two-minute pitch might be structured as follows: your *name and title*, your *mission*, a brief *success story*, and an *action request*. You probably will not have any more time in a two-minute pitch to include anything else, but go ahead and try out a few options. There are no definite rules about this, only that it must fit within two minutes and, at a minimum, contain the elements that I have described.

Conducting Meetings in a Businesslike Manner

Meetings, even though we may not want to admit it, are the hallmark of almost all businesses—nonprofit, for-profit, government agencies, etc. We all know that meetings can be extremely productive on the one hand and utterly useless on the other. It really depends on the leader of the meeting and how focused this leader is on ensuring that a meeting is productive.

As a social work manager, you can take charge of meetings and lead them in a businesslike manner. There are many different viewpoints on how to run a meeting, but put simply, according to Tropman (2006), a meeting should follow the shape of a bell in which the most difficult items occur toward the middle of the meeting when attention spans are probably the strongest. The beginning and end of a meeting should be reserved for items that may not be of utmost importance. Additionally, all meetings should have an agenda, which will help to keep all attendees (including the meeting leader) on task and focused. A sample meeting agenda is depicted in Figure 4.2. This should give you a sense of how a productive meeting is structured. Make note of the list of items, the people responsible for each item, and a time limit for each item. All of the meeting elements illustrated in Figure 4.2 can make for a more productive and businesslike meeting.

E-Mail Etiquette

E-mail is a tremendous tool for the social work manager. I will explore more thoughts about e-mail as a technology for the human services in Chapter 7. But, for now, I want to stress the importance of conducting yourself professionally with e-mail. First, e-mail messages should be as short as possible. If the e-mail cannot remain short, it may be better to pick up the phone and call the intended recipient. Also, I recommend not allowing an e-mail message, especially from one of your staff, to

Purpose of Meeting: Management Team Monthly Meeting		
Date: December 7, 2010		
Start: 9:00 a.m.		
End: 10:30 a.m.		
Location: 1 Main Street, Floor 2, Conference Room 102		
Discussion Topic	Discussion Leader(s)	Time Allotted
Executive updates	Andy	10 minutes
Program updates	Jacqueline	20 minutes
New HR policy—review, discussion, approval	Gwen	20 minutes
Conference planning updates	John and Victoria	10 minutes
Financial reports	Tanya	10 minutes
Report on new building renovations	Brian and Elena	5 minutes
Fundraising and development updates	Gerald	10 minutes
Miscellaneous business	All	5 minutes

Figure 4.2 Sample Meeting Agenda

linger for more than a day without a response. By this, I mean that you should carve out time at the end of the day to reply to all e-mails that have been sent to you in any given day. I often end up doing this later at night, but still people will appreciate that you have responded to their e-mail messages the same day. There is nothing worse, in my opinion, than sending an e-mail and waiting a long time for a reply. Sometimes the reply never comes. Finally, since e-mail is more or less a permanent record, it can be used to communicate official messages, such as the commendation message depicted in Figure 4.3. I encourage social work managers to use e-mail for formally recognizing staff members. It is easy

MARKETING, SALES, AND COMMUNICATIONS 97

From: Andy Germak

Sent: Thursday, April 14, 2011, 4:32 PM

To: mjs@socialworkservices.org

Cc: ceo@socialworkservices.org; hr@socialworkservices.org

Subject: Commendation for Recent Achievement

Dear Marcela,

I would like to commend you for your excellent work this month in securing a stable housing placement for C.F. Your diligence, dedication to our program's mission, and commitment to this particular client is duly noted. I thank you for continuing to add value to our program and I wish you continued success.

Sincerely,

Andy Germak
Program DirectorII

Figure 4.3 Sample Commendation E-mail

to do this and the message can be conveniently copied to both your supervisor and to the human resources department, as illustrated in Figure 4.3, thereby giving your staff member immediate recognition across various parts of the organization.

Recognizing and Thanking Everyone

The last area of communications on which I would like to briefly focus is the importance of giving recognition and thanks. Beyond recognizing your staff members, as explained in the last section, here I am talking about taking the time to recognize and thank those that may not frequently receive such accolades. Volunteers at your program or organization, including volunteer board members, are often deserving of attention. Vendors and other strategic partners, not to mention funders, should be routinely thanked for offering you special pricing (in the case of certain vendors) or supporting your program or organization in some capacity. As both a program manager and an executive in the human services, I have always carved out a little bit of time each week to write thank you e-mails, letters, handwritten cards, etc. to various parties that deserve thanks and recognition. Yes, sometimes handwritten cards and notes are worth the effort—people respond very well to this. Phone calls, on occasion, can also be appropriate. In the field of social work, we are infrequently recognized and thanked. I think it is our duty as social work managers and leaders to spread recognition to those who deserve it.

Chapter Summary

This chapter began with an introduction of what marketing is and what it is not, and a discussion of the common frameworks involved in the marketing process: the Four P's and STP. Next, I described the market research process and how to craft a basic marketing plan. I then focused on the sales process, which is different from, but related to, the marketing process. Both inside and outside sales strategies were introduced in relation to human service organization. The chapter concluded with an introduction to the field of communications and a few examples of communications tactics that could be helpful to social work managers.

A few important concepts from this chapter to be sure to understand are as follows:

- Marketing is more than just advertising—it is a process that involves everything necessary to bring a given product or service to market.
- The most common marketing frameworks are the Four P's (product, price, place, and promotion) and STP (segment-target-position).
- Selling is a distinct function from marketing but the two processes are highly related.
- The sales process involves selling to both internal (within your organization) and external (outside of your organization) constituents.
- Communications processes are highly correlated to both marketing and selling, and there are various communications tactics that can help the social work manager to be successful in marketing and selling.

MARKETING, SALES, AND COMMUNICATIONS 99

Suggested Learning Exercises

- Think about the main service (or product, if applicable) that is offered in the program where you work or do your field placement. Make a table similar to Table 4.1 in which you identify the Four P's (product/service, price, place, and promotion) for this main program service (or product). Provide answers to each of the questions listed in Table 4.1 in the table that you create for your program's main service.

- In a similar fashion to the exercise above, create a table that resembles Figure 4.1 in which you describe the *segments* of the market that exist for your program's main service, the *target* segment(s) within the total array of market segments on which your program is focused, and how you believe that your program's main service is *positioned* in the marketplace to attract new clients. Do prospective clients think of your program first when seeking the type of service that you offer? Why or why not? What other recommendations would you make to senior management at your organization to improve the segment-target-position framework related to your program's main service?

- Choose an issue that is currently in the "public eye" and related to the services offered by the program where you work or do your field placement. Draft a letter to the editor of your local newspaper that offers an important perspective on this issue. Remember, letters to the editor should be concise—approximately 150 words in length. Discuss this draft letter with your supervisor or field instructor and see if the organization would allow you to submit it. Do not send your letter without first getting permission from your organization!

- Develop a 30-second elevator pitch and a two-minute pitch for the program where you work or do your field placement. You may have already done part of this after reading Chapter 1. Here, you will further refine your pitch and also develop a related elevator pitch. In addition, if possible, record yourself while you deliver these pitches. If you do not like the way the video comes across, go back and rework and rerecord your pitches. If your instructor is amenable, ask if a small portion of class time can be devoted to having students stand in front of class to deliver their 30-second and two-minute pitches. Again, the key is to *practice* delivering these pitches as much as possible!

Internet Resources

NonProfit Marketing Blog—a popular blog site sponsored by Network for Good (www.networkforgood.org) that includes almost daily posts on various topics to help enhance your organization's marketing strategy: www.nonprofitmarketingblog.com.

U.S. Small Business Administration—the website of this federal government entity includes a wealth of information on marketing and sales, as well as other business-related information, which can pertain to nonprofit and public organization management. Follow this link and click on your topics of interest listed on the left-hand menu: www.sba.gov/category/navigation-structure/starting-managing-business/managing-business/running-business.

The Op-Ed Project—an initiative dedicated to increasing the range and diversity of voices and the quality of ideas in editorial media. The website contains useful resources on how to craft and pitch editorial articles: www.theopedproject.org.

Communications Consortium Media Center—a public interest group dedicated to helping nonprofits use media and new technologies effectively. The website includes tips on writing op-ed columns and letters to the editor (www.ccmc.org/node/16170), as well as submission criteria for op-ed and letter submissions to America's top 100 newspapers (www.ccmc.org/node/16170). Other useful information can be found on the organization's general website: www.ccmc.org.

The Letterbarn—a popular blog site with sample letters on a wide variety of topics. Check here for ideas on how to write commendation or other types of letters or e-mails to your staff or other stakeholders: www.letterbarn.blogspot.com.

Emailreplies.com—a simple Web-based resource providing useful information on e-mail etiquette and e-mail response management, which has become an increasing challenge in today's fast-paced social work management environment. The website also includes information on how to develop an e-mail policy for your organization: www.email replies.com.

Making Community Presentations—a publication of the Community Tool Box (http://ctb.ku.edu) at the University of Kansas, this website offers useful tips for how to plan for and deliver a formal presentation to community groups, a frequent occurrence for every social work manager: http://ctb.ku.edu/en/tablecontents/sub_section_main_1029.aspx.

Note

1. Much credit is due to John Cziepiel, professor of marketing at New York University's Stern School of Business, for first teaching me these frameworks and emphasizing their importance in the marketing process. I remember professor Cziepiel emphasizing how fundamental the segment-target-position framework was and how it would benefit us (his MBA students) in many diverse situations in our careers. Indeed, since I took his course at NYU, I have used these frameworks to help guide my marketing thinking in various human service-related contexts.

5
THE BUSINESS PLAN

Marketing plans, milestones, and pro forma financial statements—core elements of business plans—are no longer just the talk of for-profit entrepreneurs. Today, many funders in the human service sector view grants and other funding mechanisms as investments. This new way of thinking requires that social work managers develop comprehensive business plans for human service programs and show how these programs will generate returns on investment. Even public-sector government agencies are embracing business planning as a best practice in light of significant budget pressures and the need to stay focused on achieving outcomes for service recipients amid increased public scrutiny. A business plan differs somewhat from a traditional grant proposal and this chapter will attempt to point out those differences.

Specifically, this chapter will first provide a brief argument for why business planning in social work management is important, and what types of scenarios lend themselves to business planning. Next, I will explain how to assemble a business plan that communicates both social impact and financial sustainability—a "double-bottom line." The key components of a basic business plan will be presented and discussed such that you will have a framework from which to write a successful business plan for your project idea or for a new program that you seek to start. Finally, this chapter concludes with a profile of a social enterprise founded by a social worker, some discussion questions, and a copy of

The Rationale for Business Planning

Foundation and individual charitable giving markedly decreased during 2008 and 2009 (Banjo, 2010) as donors evaluated where best to invest their limited discretionary dollars during the recent economic recession, which officially ended in 2009. Although charitable giving post-recession ticked up slightly during 2010 (*Chicago Sun-Times*, 2010), and has inched even further upward during 2011 and 2012 (Linn, 2013), charitable giving remains below its pre-recession pace and, thus, competition for funding continues to be unusually strong, which has put tremendous pressure on human service organizations to sustain their essential human services in a post-recessionary environment (Thomson, 2011).

In effect, the game has clearly changed in how social work programs are funded. In addition to individual donors pulling back due to economic recession as described above, governments are significantly cutting back support that has traditionally propelled human service organizations (Nonprofit Finance Fund, 2013; The Center for Non-profits, 2013). Additionally, there are proposals presently being debated in the United States congress that could further dampen charitable giving through capping the tax deductibility of philanthropic donations made to American charities (Germak, 2013; Germak, 2012). In light of this "new normal" economy, it is evident that a new enterprising approach to financing in the social sector is needed (Wei-Skillern, Austin, Leonard, & Stevenson, 2007). If done appropriately, this business planning, social enterprising approach could even provide for enhanced social justice, better access to services, and increased equity across populations of social service beneficiaries.

A business plan is essentially a tool with which a social work manager can demonstrate capacity for sustainable program management—both the ongoing financial soundness of the program and the achievement of social outcomes from the program—and therefore raise funds from social investment-oriented funders. In addition, a business plan can serve as a roadmap with which the social work manager can launch a new social program, manage its components, and navigate its success based on milestones or benchmarks (Score Foundation, 2010). Thus, the business plan can be used for both external and internal purposes.

To help you understand some specific instances where business planning is necessary in social work management, I provide the following fictitious case vignettes, which illustrate realistic situations in which a business plan would be an essential tool for the human service organization described to achieve its programmatic objectives:

Services for the Homeless, Inc., founded in 1970, is a multi-service nonprofit organization in Chicago that helps homeless individuals and families locate stable housing and rebuild their lives. The agency employs 250 people, serves 5,000 individuals annually, and has an annual budget of $15 million. Due to recent cutbacks in its federal and state funding contracts, the agency's CEO has decided to explore the opening of a large thrift store in the center of the city as a new source of revenue for the organization. The thrift store would sell merchandise to the public and also provide employment for agency clients. The CEO needs a business plan for this project that he can present to the board of directors to show how the store would sustain itself financially and also add value to the mission of the agency.

ABC Counseling, Inc., founded in 1990, is a nonprofit organization that provides outpatient mental health counseling to individuals with low incomes in the Boston area. ABC's clients attend counseling sessions during normal business hours and most use Medicaid to cover the cost of services. The agency is located in a modern and spacious office building in the center of the city. ABC's board of directors would like to diversify funding streams and increase the agency's overall revenue given recent increases in the price of office rent. To this end, the board has asked the executive team to design a counseling program during evening and weekend hours, which would bring in more self-pay clients (at higher rates). The revenue generated from this endeavor would help offset the increasing costs of ABC's core counseling services. The executive team will need to design a business plan for this new initiative to show how the expanded program will attract and retain new paying customers and also help to support the organization's core services.

Social Services United, Inc. (SSU), a multipurpose nonprofit organization providing all types of social services to adults, children, and families in Miami, has a very talented information technology (IT) team, which has recently designed a new Web-based case management software system for the organization's internal use. This system has replaced all of the agency's paperwork; SSU has gone entirely paperless. Currently, all of SSU's case managers are required to use this system and they are giving it excellent reviews. The agency's executive director has recognized that this innovation has a lot of potential given its high quality. She would like the IT team to design an initiative to replicate and sell this system to other social service agencies in order to develop a new revenue stream for SSU. The IT team needs to craft a business plan for this new project, which will show the executive director how viable her idea is for revenue generation and, at the same time, how it will not overly tax the existing infrastructure of the organization.

Youth of Tomorrow, Inc. is a nonprofit organization in Los Angeles dedicated to improving the employment outcomes of the city's youth between the ages of 18 and 24. The organization's core service is to train youth for a variety of jobs, and then to try and place them in jobs at local corporations. Last year, the agency was able to successfully place 100 youth in full-time jobs. The agency is currently funded by foundation grants that pay for the training of the youth, but not for the job development and placement work. Therefore, Youth of Tomorrow's CEO would like to professionalize its placement operations and create a type of temporary staffing firm that would place youth in jobs that companies are seeking to fill. This way, companies would pay Youth of Tomorrow for job placements similar to how they would pay other staffing companies for temporary workers. This scenario would provide a stream of income for the agency related to its job placement work. First, the CEO will need to design a

THE BUSINESS PLAN 107

business plan before embarking on this new project to understand how this current job placement service could be brought to market and scaled up enough to provide significant revenue, while not pulling the agency away from its core social mission.

In all of the above scenarios, only a business plan would allow the organization in question to properly analyze the market, competition, pricing, and so forth for the new services being proposed. At least in theory, all of these program ideas could be worthwhile investments for a prospective funder, but the business plans would need to convince the funder of this. In addition, business plans would be used by these organizations as internal roadmaps to guide the development of these new services. Let us now turn to an overview of how to structure a basic business plan, which could be used to advance organizational objectives such as the ones mentioned above.

Basic Components of a Business Plan

The following sections describe the components of a basic social work manager's business plan, which is quite similar to a business plan used by for-profit firms. The key difference between a for-profit business plan and a social work version is that a business plan for a social work initiative contains a focus on social outcomes in addition to an emphasis on financial performance.

Although business plan formats can vary widely depending on what a particular investor requests, what the social worker entrepreneur wants to focus on, or for other reasons, a basic business plan for social work management has eight sections:

1. Executive Summary
2. Program Concept
3. Market and Competition Analysis
4. Marketing Plan
5. Operations Plan
6. Financial Plan
7. Management Team Information
8. Appendices

108   THE BUSINESS PLAN

The final plan should be approximately 30 pages in length, including all of the components as described herein. Text is typically presented single-spaced throughout the plan document. Figures and tables, especially financial spreadsheets, are usually placed within the document, not attached at the end. Again, these are guidelines intended to help you craft a basic business plan. Formats do vary, and you may be asked by a prospective investor or funder to add, change, or edit certain sections of your plan. The length of your plan may also vary depending on what is requested, if such instructions are available.

Executive Summary

The executive summary is an opportunity to make the initial sales pitch for your particular social work program idea. Remember the focus on developing sales pitches discussed in Chapters 1 and 4—this is also an important skill for business planning.

Ideally, the executive summary should be about one page in length. If it needs to be a bit longer to capture all of the necessary information, it can be, but the executive summary should be no longer than two pages, maximum. A basic rule of thumb is if you cannot summarize your program idea in less than five minutes, your summary is too long. It is important to realize that this will most likely be the first section that investors or funders will look at in your business plan. If the executive summary sparks some interest, they may read further. If it does not, then all of your other efforts may be for naught. Often, it is easiest to write this section last after all the other business plan components have been completed and understood. Nonetheless, it is essential that the executive summary include the following components written in a concise and engaging style in order to capture the reader's attention:

- Brief description of the basic program concept.
- Overview of market size and proposed opportunity to capture market share.
- Discussion of key competition that is anticipated.
- General plan to make money and achieve social impact.
- A more specific description of how your new program will create social impact (e.g. how is it different from a commercial business?).

THE BUSINESS PLAN   109

- Brief management biographies of key leaders—thumbnail highlights only.

Program Concept

In this section, there is an opportunity to delve deeper into the details of the program concept. For those interested in launching products instead of services, this section would be quite similar but would be used to describe the product concept instead of the program or service idea. It is important to understand the program concept in the context of the entire market that exists for your type of program. That is, there must be a demonstrated and strong grasp of the industry in which the program resides, as well as knowledge of the history of the particular program service and its success or failure and why it did or did not succeed. The following components should be included in this section, which should be between two and four pages in length in total. You may choose to use graphics to explain some these items:

- Description of program service (or product in some cases, as applicable).
- Description of industry in which program will operate.
- Overview and capacity of organization launching the new program.
- History of program service (or product) throughout the industry.
- Description of the market opportunity and market share available.
- Explanation of program milestones. How and when, based on your estimation, will the venture or program achieve both financial and social impact success? How are you defining social impact (more on this in Chapter 6)?

Market and Competition Analysis

This section differs considerably from the needs assessments that some social work managers may have experience writing in more traditional grant proposals. The key idea here is that a business plan is based on customer demand, not necessarily need, which is dictated by looking at the potential market for a particular service and making some estimate of demand for the program service: do people want this new service and what would they be willing to pay for it? This is different from an assessment of need in which a professional determines what a population needs, not always what the population necessarily wants or is demanding. Here, the emphasis is on what a customer wants and is willing to pay for, which may not always be the same as what the customer needs (and may not be willing to pay for). Very often, this section is based on customized marketing surveys and primary data collected from the prospective market. Thus, before writing this section of the business plan, you may need to conduct some preliminary research if data are not available to you in these specific categories.

Also important to include in this section is a brief analysis of the competition that exists in the marketplace for your service or product and a description of the strategy you will use to gain competitive advantage—to be the best and most utilized program in the marketplace. It may be helpful to think about Porter's generic strategies (Porter, 1980, 1985) when deciding on an appropriate strategy for your new program. Porter's generic strategies are cost leadership, differentiation, and focus. Cost leadership essentially means that you will compete on price and offer the best price available to the customer for comparable quality in the market. Differentiation is a strategy in which your program will be so unique and unparalleled in the market that customers must choose it. Focus-type strategies are somewhat of a combination of the previous two, but with an emphasis on a very particular segment of the market. By focusing closely on a market segment, your program can gain market share due to its close understanding of the demands of a particular market segment. Therefore, the following items should be expanded upon in this section:

- Demonstration of market demand for new program based on available data.
- Who are the customers, clients, donors, etc. that you plan to target?
- Market share, size, and trends—expansion from previous business plan section.
- Estimated willingness of customers to pay (or investors to fund) based on available data or historical evidence.

THE BUSINESS PLAN 111

- Value added, customer benefits, problems solved because of new program.
- Analysis of your program's competition. Who are your closest competitors and what do they offer that is similar? What makes your program offering different?
- Statement of competitive advantage. How and why will your new program outperform, in the sense of gaining more customers, similar programs already in the market?

Marketing Plan

In this section, a marketing plan or a roadmap is presented as to how the program idea will be brought to market and actually sold to customers, clients, donors, and the like. In other words, the business plan up to this point should have successfully presented the program concept and explained the demand that exists in the marketplace for the particular program concept. Now, the business plan must effectively explain how the idea will connect with the market, fill the market demand, and capture a substantial share of the market to make the program viable and worthwhile for investment. A marketing plan within a business plan document can take a variety of forms. Some marketing plans alone may be dozens of pages long for very complex products in global marketplaces. As specified in Chapter 4, a stand-alone marketing plan for a human service program or organization should be five to six pages ideally. However, to keep things simple, a concise marketing plan for a social program idea that is housed within a business plan document should discuss the following frameworks (these were introduced in more detail in Chapter 4) in two to three pages. The use of figures and tables may be helpful in describing some of the following items:

Segment-Target-Position (STP) Framework

- Segment—describe the various segments of the market that could potentially be drawn to your new program.
- Target—select a segment on which to focus with your new program and describe your reasoning for this choice.
- Position—describe how your new program will be optimally situated in the marketplace to capture and maintain the target segment described.

The Four P's Framework

- Product (or service)—what is being pitched to the market?
- Price—how much will it cost?
- Place—where will it be offered?
- Promotion—how will customers know about the service?

Operations Plan

So far, the business plan has not focused on how the social work manager or organization will actually execute the program concept. Up to this point in the document, there should have been ample discussion about what this program concept is, how the marketplace looks for the introduction of your program concept, and how the new program will be effectively marketed (e.g. sold) to the marketplace. But what are the actual mechanics of the proposed program? How does it work? How does the overall organization execute the program if you are launching it as a project of a larger agency? These questions need to be answered succinctly in this section of the business plan, which should be about two to three pages in length, and should include the following:

- Description of how program works. What are the mechanics necessary to carry out all aspects of the new program?
- Operating cycle (timeline and schedule) for the program—can be week by week, month by month, or some other schedule based on the design of the proposed program.
- Logistics—locations of services, details on the delivery of product or service (if applicable), manufacturing process (if applicable), etc.
- Human resource strategy and plan for acquiring and maintaining talent.
- Discussion of regulatory and legal issues as necessary.

Financial Plan

The financial plan section of the business plan document is probably the most important to portray clearly and realistically. Together with the executive summary, the financial plan may represent a key decision point for investors and funders interested in your program idea. It is not uncommon for an interested investor to flip through the business plan—before reading anything except the executive summary—and take a look at the financial viability of the proposed idea. The financial plan section should be presented with both financial projections in the form of a spreadsheet (see Figure 2.10 in Chapter 2 as an example of a pro forma income statement) and with a narrative explaining the numbers in the spreadsheet and how they were derived. Altogether, this section should encompass two to three pages of the entire business plan document. Some investors and funders will require more detailed financial statements once they express some initial interest in a project. For the initial business plan, however, remember to always include the following key elements:

- Start-up funds required and planned use—can be explained in a narrative format.
- Historical financial statements going back five years, if available.
- Ideally, five-year pro forma projections for new program—include, if possible, the following financial statements in pro forma:
  — Income statement
  — Statement of cash flows
  — Balance sheet

Management Team Information

Almost always, funders and investors want to know more about the key managers and personnel that will be the custodians of the financial investment. It is important to investors to understand that the management team is not only entrepreneurial and innovative, but also capable of managing investments, which in many cases are large sums of money that need to be managed appropriately. Therefore, a business plan should include bio sketches of all of the key personnel, which should include the board of directors and the top management team (see the end of this chapter for a helpful Internet resource on writing your bio sketch and also refer to my professional bio sketch at the start of this book, which may be a helpful example). In addition, if there are program personnel important to the execution of the business plan further down in the agency structure, they should also be included in this section. Investors will be interested in what type of total compensation (salary, benefits, etc.) is being offered to the management, which can help them understand whether the funds that are being requested are sufficient enough to support the necessary talent for the venture. Finally, an organizational chart can help to pictorially explain reporting relationships in more complex organizations. The following is a list of what should be included in this section, not to exceed five pages in length:

- Biographical sketches of key management personnel.
- Board of directors listing/biographical sketches.
- Management and key personnel compensation (and ownership structure if for-profit company).
- Organizational chart.

Appendices

Finally, certain situations may require that various documents be appended to the back of the business plan document. When possible, this section should be limited to five pages so that the entire business plan is approximately 30 pages in length or shorter. Some items that may be important to include as appendices are the following, as appropriate to your specific program idea:

- References/bibliography as cited or utilized throughout the business plan.
- Curricula vitae (CVs) or resumes of key management personnel.
- Relevant media articles about your organization or about your management capabilities.
- Product specifications, if applicable.
- Geospatial mappings—useful for showing locations of services in a community.
- Miscellaneous charts and tables, as needed.

In short, basic business plans are comprised of the above sections and subsections. You may want to structure your business plan document using the actual sections and subsections presented in this chapter as your headings and subheadings in your business plan document. Table 5.1

Table 5.1 Business Plan Format Summary

Plan Section	General Purpose of Section	Suggested Length
Executive summary	• The "sales pitch" for your project idea	One to two pages
Venture/program concept	• Product/service description and background	Two to four pages
Market analysis	• Description of marketplace, customer demand, willingness to pay, competition, etc.	Two to three pages
Marketing plan	• Roadmap for how product or service will be introduced to marketplace • STP and Four P's frameworks	Two to three pages
Operations plan	• How you and your organization will execute all aspects of the business plan	Two to three pages
Financial plan	• Five-year pro forma, as applicable: income statement, balance sheet, statement of cash flows • Narrative and spreadsheets	Two to three pages
Management team	• Board and top management composition and proposed organizational structure	Up to five pages
Appendices	• References, CVs, media articles, etc.	Up to five pages

provides a quick snapshot of each of these sections, its purpose, and its suggested length in the overall business plan document.

Perspectives from the Field: Business Planning in a Social Work Setting

For approximately one year, I have been working with Patty Mojta, a recent graduate of the MSW program at Rutgers University, to create and revise a business plan for a new social venture that she has developed. The venture is called Parent Universe and it is a profit-making subsidiary of Prevent Child Abuse New Jersey, Inc., a nonprofit human service organization dedicated to advocacy and preventive services throughout the state of New Jersey. Patty's executive director and the board of directors of her agency have been quite supportive of her conceiving of and launching this social venture. In addition, in 2012, Patty was chosen as a fellow of the New Jersey Social Innovation Institute at Rutgers Business School-Newark and New Brunswick, where she spent over six months learning the various aspects of business planning and received technical assistance with her new venture.

I would like to share with you a profile of Parent Universe, some questions for discussion, and a complete business plan for this venture. All of these items are included in the appendices, which follow the final chapter of this book.

Chapter Summary

The primary aim of this chapter was to introduce business planning to social work managers. Specifically, this chapter reviewed the need for business planning in today's competitive human service environment. Next, I provided a framework for writing a basic business plan for a social program concept, and reviewed the necessary contents for each section of a basic business plan document. The chapter also introduced a profile of an entrepreneurial program founded by a social work manager and presented the business plan for this program for your study and reference (these items are included in the appendices to this book). In conclusion, it is clear that today's social problems require new management solutions amid a constrained economic environment, and business planning can be a key tool in this regard.

A few important concepts from this chapter to be sure to understand are as follows:

- Business planning, once only a process known to for-profit organizations, is becoming commonplace in human service organizations and, in fact, social work managers are being asked by funders to create business plans for programs and organizations as opposed to more traditional applications for grant funding.
- The main difference between a social work-type business plan and a commercial business plan is that the former focuses on not only financial viability, but also social impact—the degree to which the social problems addressed are resolved.
- A business plan for a social work program or organization should be approximately 30 pages in length and include the following eight components (refer to Appendix 3 of this book for a sample business plan): (1) executive summary; (2) program concept; (3) market and competition analysis; (4) marketing plan; (5) operations plan; (6) financial plan; (7) management team info; and (8) appendices.

Suggested Learning Exercises

- Early in this chapter, four case vignettes were presented for the following fictitious organizations: Services for the Homeless, ABC Counseling, Social Services United, and Youth of Tomorrow. In a team of two to five people, review the details provided in one of the case vignettes. Make assumptions as needed for information that is not explicitly stated. Then, create a bullet-pointed executive summary for the business idea presented in the case. Choose one spokesperson from your team to present, in two minutes or less, the executive summary to the rest of the class.
- One of the most important concepts that differentiate business plans from more traditional fundraising and grant writing is the analysis of competition. Think about the program where you work or do your field placement and write the *market analysis and*

competition section of a potential business plan for this program. As you write, consider what competition exists in the marketplace for your program's services and how you can establish competitive advantage in this marketplace.

- Create a bio sketch for yourself that you could include in a business plan or for other professional use. As a reference and to help you get started, visit the website below ("The Seven Steps to Creating a Professional Bio"), which will show you how to develop your professional bio sketch. After you develop your bio sketch, you may want to post it as a summary on your LinkedIn profile (see "Suggested Learning Exercises" from Chapter 3).

- Obtain a quarterly income statement for the program or agency where you work or do your field placement. Create a five-year pro forma income statement based on the statement that you obtain (refer to Figure 2.10 in Chapter 2, as needed). Remember to use the process of annualizing (see sections on annualizing revenue and expense in Chapter 2) to move from quarterly to annual figures. Also, if you are unable to obtain a quarterly income statement, you can make up the numbers based on reasonable assumptions. What sources of revenue exist? What are the assumed expenses? The most important part of this exercise is not obtaining the quarterly income statement (that was a key objective of the exercise from Chapter 2), but rather practicing how to create a pro forma (forward-looking) income statement for five years based on a current quarterly income statement.

Internet Resources

The Roberts Enterprise Development Fund (REDF)—an intermediary venture philanthropy-type organization that funds and helps to develop social enterprises. The website contains business planning and other helpful tools. Registration is free, but necessary to access the tools: www.redf.org.

Berkley Center for Entrepreneurship and Innovation—a leading academic center housed within the Stern School of Business at New York

University, the Berkley Center offers many services and programs to the entrepreneurship community, including an annual social venture business plan competition where you can compete for prize money for your social venture idea, and an annual conference for social entrepreneurs: www. stern.nyu.edu/experience-stern/about/departments-centers-initiatives/ centers-of-research/berkley-center/index.htm.

SCORE—an organization supported by the U.S. Small Business Administration that helps small businesses to develop across the United States. Among many useful tools available for free download, the website contains a business planning toolkit for nonprofit organizations (www. score.org/resources/business-planning-tools-nonprofit-organizations). Other information, articles, and tools are available here: www.score.org.

The Seven Steps to Writing a Professional Bio—a very useful template for crafting a succinct and professional biography about yourself to include in a business plan document (or for other reasons): http://umassalumni. com/career-blog/2011/10/the-seven-steps-to-writing-a-professional-bio/.

Resumes and Vitas—Purdue University's Online Writing Lab contains good information on how to construct your resume or curriculum vitae for use in business plans, or for general job-searching purposes: http:// owl.english.purdue.edu/owl/section/6/23/.

Compensation Advice for Nonprofits—Pete Smith, former president, CEO, and chairman of Watson Wyatt Worldwide (now known as Towers Watson), a global human resource consulting firm, now runs a boutique consultancy and maintains a blog geared toward nonprofits. A good resource for making compensation decisions for your business plan or otherwise: www.nonprofitmusings.com.

6

IMPACT, SUSTAINABILITY, AND EFFECTIVENESS/PERFORMANCE MEASUREMENT

"Are we seeking to measure something that is even possible to measure, or are we just spinning our wheels to find a standard measurement for impact and sustainability, and a way to carry out meaningful performance measurement for the human services and for social programs?" This was a frustrated question from an audience member during a panel entitled "Evaluation: Current Trends and Challenges" that I attended at the 2011 annual conference of the Association for Research on Nonprofit Organizations and Voluntary Action (ARNOVA). To be sure, in recent years, especially since the advent of heightened accountability among human service programs of all types, scholars of human service management, social work management practitioners, and funders have debated the definitions of social impact, sustainability, and what program and organizational performance or effectiveness measurement should look like in the nonprofit and public human service sectors (Maas & Liket, 2011; Brown, 2010; Carman, 2011). Unfortunately, there is no established "gold standard" measure for overall effectiveness in this space such as in the for-profit or corporate sector in which financial return metrics are often used as a gauge of a company's performance or effectiveness. As the question raised at the recent ARNOVA conference indicates, there is a certain level of general disagreement, or at least confusion, over how these issues should be approached in both research and in practice.

122   EFFECTIVENESS/PERFORMANCE MEASUREMENT

Some social work managers and scholars may wonder whether program or organizational performance measurement even matters in the human service sector, especially among nonprofit human service organizations. After all, such organizations are charitable agencies designed first and foremost to provide services to those in need, right? Serving those in need most often seems like the most important objective, so why focus on other, less central objectives? Taking an extreme view, why should we bother with performance measurement at all, especially, as Pallotta (2008) describes, since measuring performance by way of financial metrics alone (assuming that is all that we can do well) has little to do with how a charitable organization is helping society, fulfilling its charitable mission, or creating social impact?

Still, although performance measurement has its critics and is by no means perfect, the pressure on human service organizations—both public and nonprofit—to be financially sustainable, carry out their charitable missions effectively, and measure and report their social impact has never been greater (Lynch-Cerullo & Cooney, 2011; Carman, 2009). Therefore, it is indeed important to dedicate a small part of this book to trying to understand these concepts and move our thinking forward. This chapter will not fully resolve the confusion over performance measurement in the social work space, but, ultimately, it should underscore how an increased and continual focus on these issues could lead to the development of a more standard metric of measuring the impact of social work programs and organizations.

Thus, this chapter will begin with a brief discussion of how social impact and financial sustainability are commonly defined. I will then discuss the ways in which different types of organizations typically measure performance or the effectiveness of their programs or of the overall organization. An explanation of the logic model as an important tool for attempting to measure performance along the social impact dimension will then follow. The chapter will conclude with excerpts from an interview with a social work manager who leads an established social enterprise-type human service organization and must frequently focus on how to measure the impact and sustainability of his organization's programs.

Defining Impact, Sustainability, and Effectiveness/Performance

The literature on human service program and organizational health or well-being uses a variety of terminology to describe the central concepts of effectiveness or performance—how well a human service program or organization addresses the social problem or problems that it sets out to solve through its core mission. Social impact can essentially be thought of as the change that a program or organization makes to a client, group of clients, family unit, community, society, etc. in a non-monetary way. Financial sustainability, on the other hand, is concerned with how well a program or organization is able to generate sufficient revenue to provide its services without interruption. Hence, social impact finds itself at the opposite end of the program or organizational well-being spectrum, so to speak, from financial performance. Social impact is concerned with the non-monetary value added while financial sustainability refers to monetary value added, in a sense. It should be noted that sustainability can also be conceptualized along the environmental dimension—how well a program or organization is able to maintain (or at least not destroy) the physical environment. While this idea is indeed important and deserving of attention, when I discuss sustainability in this chapter, I am referring specifically to financial sustainability, which is ultimately more of a concern for human service organizations at present than environmental sustainability is. Perhaps once we conquer the problem of financial sustainability in our field, we can move on to the environmental dimension!

In discussing and trying to best define the concept of performance, which is also known as effectiveness, it is helpful to first review and understand the following terminology before proceeding. First of all, the phrase *firm performance* is almost never used in the human services or social work literature, especially when referring to public-sector entities. Firms or companies in the social work sphere are referred to as organizations or charities, even though nonprofit organizations can indeed be legally incorporated and look much like for-profit firms on the surface (Patti, 2009). Moreover, the term *performance* is often replaced by the word *effectiveness* or sometimes just the word *impact* in the literature on these topics. Because of this, it is very important to try to understand

124 EFFECTIVENESS/PERFORMANCE MEASUREMENT

what a scholar or practitioner is actually talking about when these terms are used. Generally speaking, it is common in the social work sphere to see the phrase *program/organizational effectiveness*, which is nearly equivalent to the phrase *firm performance*, a phrase commonly used in the strategic management literature and in for-profit management practice, for example. All of these concepts are related to the term *social impact* in the sense that, at least in human the human service domain, programs and organizations cannot be effective or perform well without some focus on positive social outcomes. Indeed, in social work organizations, it is equally important that there be *financial sustainability* of the various programs or of the organization as a whole. Thus, impact and sustainability together constitute performance or effectiveness in the human service sector. Lastly, the concept of *program evaluation* (or simply *evaluation*) is frequently discussed in the nonprofit and public management literature. Notwithstanding all that I mention in this paragraph, it is very important to keep in mind that, at least from an academic standpoint (Herman & Renz, 2008; Wang, 2002), the concept of organizational performance or at the program level, program effectiveness, among human service organizations and how it gets measured continues to be vigorously debated in the literature.

The focus of this chapter is on all of the above related concepts. This may at first seem confusing, but I cannot emphasize enough that much of the literature on this topic is similarly confusing; more academic work is required to bring much needed clarity to this topic. For the purposes of this chapter and your learning, it is important to understand that the precise meanings of impact, sustainability, effectiveness, and performance may differ depending on context, and they can refer to total organizational health, the individual well-being of programs or projects, or some other benchmark upon which a human service organization's mission is measured. Also, keep in mind that social impact is distinct from financial sustainability. These two components of program or organizational effectiveness working together constitute the ultimate measure of human service effectiveness, which has yet to be concisely defined.

Measuring Program or Organizational Effectiveness/Performance

Although it may be theoretically difficult to define program or organizational effectiveness, it is still necessary to measure it as practicing social work managers. The first step in measurement should be to define as best you can what you intend to accomplish by carrying out your program or running your organization. As Kickul and Lyons (2012) describe it, this is your social value proposition or the nature of the contribution your program or organization intends to make to the community or to society at large. This is essentially the reason you are in the social work business as opposed to another type of business.

If you are running a program within a larger organization, your social value proposition may or may not be equivalent to the core mission of your organization. A human service organization with a mission aimed at eliminating homelessness in the city of Chicago, for example, might operate a variety of programs under its umbrella. The measurement of effectiveness or performance of the entire agency may very well be different from the measurements used across its programs. Imagine for a moment that one of this agency's programs is a soup kitchen whose primary goal is to provide breakfast, lunch, and dinner to families in a certain Chicago neighborhood on a daily basis. This program may wish to measure the outputs of its operations as the number of meals served in a particular week or month. It may further break down these meal counts by the number of breakfasts, lunches, and dinners. It may in turn choose to measure its outcomes as enhancements in nutritional health experienced by the clients that frequent the soup kitchen in that particular neighborhood. I will discuss outputs versus outcomes in more detail in the next section, but for the purposes of this example, it is sufficient to understand how this soup kitchen's programs would approach performance measurement (for a comparison of outputs versus outcomes, please refer to Table 6.1). The larger agency in this example would most definitely seek to measure broader outcomes of reduced homelessness and so forth. Program performance measurements should relate to overall organizational performance measurements, but they are not always identical, especially for larger organizations.

Outputs versus Outcomes

Often, as I alluded to previously, funders and other important stakeholders place demands on social work managers to routinely measure outputs and outcomes of the programs and organizations that they oversee. On many occasions, either formally or informally, as a program and organizational leader, I have been asked to provide measurement statistics and have responded to funders' requests for data from programs that I have overseen. Often, it appears that there might be little concern for the true well-being of clients during these exercises; funders, especially, are usually only seeking data (i.e. numbers), which tell a story of how you are creating social impact through your work. Nonetheless, it is essential to understand that most funders and other stakeholders do have the best interests of clients in mind, and it is important as a social worker to not lose focus on this primary issue. If the measurement process veers too far from a focus on client outcomes, it is incumbent upon the social work manager to address this issue with the necessary stakeholders. According to Gill (2010), nonprofit organizations can easily and often lose sight of outcomes and the intended mission of the organization, especially when feeling outside pressure from stakeholders, which is why consistent measurement and feedback on progress is important to the ongoing effectiveness of an organization. Organizations can facilitate regular impact meetings, for example, in which leadership and staff together discuss how various outcomes are being measured throughout the organization. If you make measurement and performance improvement an integral part of your organizational culture, these exercises become incorporated into the routine business processes of an organization.

Indeed, it is often paramount that certain types of organizations make measurement an ingrained and institutionalized aspect of the organization. Brooks (2009) insists that social entrepreneurs—I would include businesslike social work managers in this category—must try to precisely measure outcomes because it gives their work legitimacy. Social enterprise programs and organizations can easily be confused with commercial enterprises due to their dual focus on social impact and financial performance or sustainability. Funders, donors, and investors in social enterprises would much prefer to finance solutions that can prove their

EFFECTIVENESS/PERFORMANCE MEASUREMENT   127

Table 6.1 Outputs versus Outcomes

Program Type	Output Example	Outcome Example
Job Training	• Employers in community are informed about training program	• Employers formally partner with agency to offer jobs to clients on ongoing basis
Counseling	• Client (or family) attends scheduled counseling session on time and actively participates	• Client (or family) demonstrates enhanced functioning, well-being, etc. after attending session
Parenting Education	• New parenting course achieves maximum enrollment of new parents	• Parenting behaviors in the local community improve after the course is offered
Child Protection	• Caseworker makes required number of home visits each week in assigned neighborhood	• Child abuse and neglect occurrences decline in the caseworker's assigned area
Policy Advocacy	• Hundreds of phone calls are made to local legislators during an advocacy campaign	• The targeted legislation is passed (or blocked) as desired by the advocacy group

social value rather than those that are mysterious or elusive in this area, or those that simply prove a financial return. It is incumbent upon social entrepreneurs to communicate about social impact to all involved stakeholders.

The challenge for social work managers when conducting performance measurement often becomes one of distinguishing between outputs and outcomes (Lynch-Cerullo & Cooney, 2011). According to Sandfort (2010), a human service organization typically provides services to clients and through these services produces both outputs and eventually outcomes. Outputs are process driven and transactional in nature, and are often measured by examining available quantitative data. For instance, how many clients have gone through a particular program? What was the cost per client for this program? How long did it take for the client to complete the program? What are the levels of service that were achieved by a program during a given period of time? It is usually easy to find answers to these questions by looking at available client data. Essentially, these are questions based on the processes with which a human service organization carries out its charitable work (or its social impact work in the case of a for-profit human service organization).

Still, these questions do not address whether clients are better off having gone through the organization's programs, or whether the organization's programs have alleviated the social problems they were designed to address. Such issues are referred to as impact or outcome measurements, a much different construct from process or output measurements (Murray, 2010), which are easier to operationalize. Nonetheless, process measurements (outputs) of program or organizational performance are important and part of the overall performance measurement picture (Martin & Kettner, 1997). Moreover, such measures are frequently reported and serve as a way of comparing similar types of programs or organizations. Table 6.1 illustrates examples of outputs and outcomes for five different program types commonly seen in the social work field: job training, counseling, parenting education, child protection, and policy advocacy. Chances are, you can fit the program where you work or do your field placement with one of these sample program types to see whether your program or organization is focused on outputs, outcomes, or some combination of both.

In summary, further theoretical work is necessary to combine process performance, or outputs, with client outcomes to develop a more comprehensive understanding of human service program or organizational performance. At present, as a field, we seem to have mediocre measurements of client outcomes that have been developed and somewhat decent measures of outputs processes. We have almost no good combined measurement tools for outputs and outcomes taken together. Furthermore, attempting to combine social impact and financial sustainability into one overall metric proves to be even more challenging. These would be tremendous developments in the social work field and very worthy of further study and attention.

EFFECTIVENESS/PERFORMANCE MEASUREMENT 129

How For-Profit Organizations Measure Effectiveness/Performance

I think it is instructive to examine for a moment a sector in which effectiveness and performance measurement is a robust and widely standardized practice. Companies in the for-profit sector expend much energy on this practice, although, as you will see, its measures are simpler and easier to operationalize. Remember from Chapter 1 that for-profit organizations are ultimately designed to benefit the owners or shareholders of the organization. Thus, in the classic sense, for-profit organizations are concerned with maximizing profits so that these individuals or groups can reap the monetary rewards of the organization's performance. In this scenario, for-profit organizations would measure their performance or effectiveness—more commonly referred to as company or firm performance—by way of financial metrics. For example, return on assets (ROA) is a common metric used by for-profit companies to measure overall company performance. This measure is typically reported as a percentage and can be used across similar organizations to compare performance. Recall from Chapter 2 that assets are items that are in a sense owned by an organization. Therefore, return on assets would represent the amount of money earned by the organization in relation to the assets it owns. Another way of looking at this would be to say that a certain amount of profit is derived from the assets of the company. The more money earned by an organization per asset level, the more valuable the organization would be from a purely financial or investment standpoint. In turn, such an organization may have an easier time attracting outside investment. There are several other commonly used performance metrics in the for-profit world, such as return on equity, return on sales, sales per square foot, and so forth. All of these are focused on the financial performance of the underlying firm.

This does not mean that for-profit organizations completely shun non-financial performance indicators. It is common, for instance, for for-profits to report on customer or employee satisfaction, energy savings from operations, levels of innovation, reputational ranking, and so forth. However, I would argue that, ultimately, all performance measures used by for-profit organizations—whether overtly financial or otherwise—in some way relate to the financial health of the organization. An exception to this trend would be some of the new for-profit organizational legal forms, such as benefit corporations (i.e. B-corps) that must, by law, measure both financial sustainability and social impact performance. But these legal forms are still emerging and do not represent the majority of for-profit organizations nor do they reflect how performance is typically measured in the for-profit sector.

Is Effectiveness/Performance Measurement of Social Work Programs and Organizations Possible?

Performance measurement in the human service sector is not without its critics. Ridley-Duff and Bull (2011) take a critical view of effectiveness measurement in claiming that the commercialization of the human service sector negates the immeasurable social value that is created by these types of services. As these and other scholars often argue, some outcomes of human service programs are not easily measureable. How, for instance, do we measure the value added to a community by reductions in homelessness, to extend our discussion of the example presented earlier in this chapter? Do we look at the increased property values in the area? Do we instead examine happiness, well-being, or overall health of a neighborhood's inhabitants? Do we consider some other measures of program success? These questions are not easily answered, but thinking in this manner allows us to see just how complicated it can be to measure the performance of programs and organizations.

Some of the criticism of measurement in the social work space is quite pronounced. Well-known nonprofit activist and consultant Dan Pallotta is adamant that we cannot measure the effectiveness of human service organizations by examining financial metrics alone, which only tell us about the efficiency of an organization or program (Pallotta, 2008, 2012).

Still, others posit that financial measures, which can be typically observed by way of Internal Revenue Service (IRS) data or the audited financial statements that some organizations release, serve as good proxies for the performance of an organization (Ritchie & Kolodinsky, 2003; Tekula, 2010). Financial efficiency, it is argued, represents a healthy organization that is efficiently using its available resources to carry out its programs and services. These types of measurement techniques are attempts at overlaying a for-profit mentality onto a nonprofit or public-sector service environment.

However, using only financial efficiency as a proxy for overall organizational performance misses a key component of performance measurement in the social work sector—how does an organization actually measure whether it has fulfilled its charitable mission? Oster (1995) posits that since no market exists that can communicate sufficient information regarding the total value of a human service organization, the measurement of program or organizational performance must go beyond output-level data, such as financial metrics that are reported in an organization's financial statements. Ultimately, good measurement must combine social impact *and* financial sustainability metrics.

Complicating the issue of performance measurement even further, Brown (2010) argues that, quite often, certain groups within and external to human service organizations may resist or implicitly control the performance measurement process. For instance, some private foundations refuse to contribute funding toward administrative overhead expenses of a nonprofit human service organization. Thus, when such an organization reports its performance to this funder, it may show little to no overhead expense, which is most likely not a reflection of reality; organizations do need to spend significant money on overhead in order to achieve their charitable missions (Pallotta, 2008). Furthermore, Murray (2010) extends this argument by claiming that performance measurement in the nonprofit sector is inherently political and organizations respond to political forces of their stakeholders when assessing and reporting their program or organizational performance.

Essentially, the process of program or organizational performance measurement in the human service sector is currently more subjective than objective, which results in much variation in performance data available from organizations. Additionally, because human service organizations often report performance data in response to certain pressures or political forces, it is not clear that the performance data is a reliable indicator of the actual effectiveness or performance of the organization.

Using Logic Models to Guide the Measurement Process

Despite the fact that the program and organizational performance measurement process in the human service sector is imperfect, an important tool exists for mapping out program or organizational outputs and outcomes. This tool is called a logic model. Logic models are often requested by funders when applying for funding for a new or existing program.

A logic model essentially describes, in a graphical format, the logic or flow of a program or organization. On the left side of the logic model are inputs to the program or organizational system. In the middle of the model are the activities that occur inside of the program or organization. Finally, on the right side of the model are the expected outputs and outcomes of the program or organization.

Figure 6.1 contains a sample logic model. Note that the inputs to the system include everything that is needed to operate the program or organization, including clients, staff, volunteers, and so forth. Next, during the operation of this program or organization, these inputs move through the activities section of the logic model. There, a client would partake in a program or a service, for example. A volunteer would receive necessary training, and so on. Finally, these activities produce outputs and outcomes. Outputs are more proximal and are immediate results of program or organizational activities, such as the levels of service reported by a program, for instance. Outcomes are more distal and include the ultimate social impact measures that the program or organization is seeking, such as achievement of program goals or of the agency mission. If you have more interest in using logic models in your work or in your field placement, there is a more complex logic model based on an actual

Figure 6.1 Sample Logic Model

social enterprise included as part of the business plan for Parent Universe, which can be found in Appendix 3 of this book (the logic model for this program is included toward the end of the business plan document).

Perspectives from the Field: Impact, Sustainability, and Measurement

The following is an interview with Wendell Knight, MSW, LMSW, a social entrepreneur who leads what he calls a social purpose business, MTI Business Development, Inc., dedicated to helping veterans with various barriers ready themselves for employment and obtain jobs. I asked Wendell several questions pertaining to his business and how he defines the social impact and financial sustainability of his work. The following excerpts from our interview should help to illustrate some of the concepts introduced earlier in this chapter, especially as they pertain to a businesslike or entrepreneurial social work organization.

What is the mission or purpose of MTI Business Development, Inc.?
Our core focus is on enhancing the well-being of veterans by providing internships and employment opportunities for veterans with various barriers. We accomplish this through operating enterprises open to the public, such as a café, that are commercial in nature. We train and employ our veterans with barriers in these enterprises.

MTI is a so-called social purpose business. What are your thoughts about financial objectives, which seem inherent to this business?
I think that revenue objectives may frighten certain people. I purposely didn't include that in the mission or in our core values. It may turn off foundations and funders. Actually, I rarely talk about that even though it is extremely important to our operations. I think that, depending on the audience, financial objectives and performance on that dimension is something that you need to slowly bring in to the conversation when doing this work.

In your opinion, how is MTI different (or similar) to nonprofit human service organizations?
You've got to be a pioneer when running an impact-driven organization. Usually, it's an uphill battle all the way. MTI may

not be much different in look and feel from a more well-known entrepreneurial service organization like the Girl Scouts, but what Girl Scouts did along the way was change their product. Product quality drives a service business like ours. I don't think the classic Girl Scout cookie is as good anymore. It used to be much better. In contrast, here, I am determined to sell the best barbeque food through our café operation and be consistent with that into the future. We are known by many people for the quality of our food. I don't think this organization should become gigantic because I might literally lose the flavor and lose sight of the reasons why I got into the business in the first place. So perhaps the big difference between what I do and the typical human service organization is that we don't want to grow huge—small is better in our opinion. Instead, our board and staff team needs to consist of passionate people. This is what will keep us going ultimately because from this our total performance will be inspired and continue to be enhanced.

How would you define social impact in the context of your organization?
My thoughts on this start with our initial engagements with the veterans that we serve. They must realize that they are the most important people to our organization right from our initial engagement . . . right from the beginning. We need to give them dignity and help them feel valuable and important or none of this will work. I think that much of the social work world is forgetting about this idea. Many social work programs and organizations are so focused on the number of visits, levels of service, etc. These programs lose sight of the person, I feel. So, beyond this initial impact definition, in our work, we want to ensure that an individual's career plan and goals are supported. We shouldn't be judgmental about their career plans or goals— they are our most important customer in a sense.

How do you measure the social impact of your programs?
We measure impact on a variety of levels. During our initial intake interviews, we write down key things about family

connections or lack thereof, for example. Then, we measure, at various intervals during the course of our programs, how we are doing at reconnecting veterans to their families. We are not just focused on employment goals or the number of months before obtaining employment, for example, because it isn't that simple. Working with veterans with barriers means that you look at everything, literally. For some of our folks, housing is the biggest barrier. It can be such an important prerequisite, if you will, to one's career objectives. So, in some cases, we measure progress toward various housing goals. Case managers by default do much of our impact measurement in our programs because they meet regularly with our clients.

What are your thoughts on financial sustainability and how important is financial sustainability to human service programs in general? It depends on what part of an organization's components you are looking at. To me, there are all kinds of sustainability in organizations. It could be sustainability in funding. It might be human resource-related . . . or something else. In my business, I need to look at more than just financial sustainability—I have to look at overall impact—because even with lots of money, I can't meet outcomes if I am just thinking about finances. This is the nature of a social purpose business . . . of a social venture. Do typical nonprofits think like this? In my experience, the answer is no. When an org is formed with lots of grant money, you don't think about these things. This is not a good scenario either.

What do you wish you learned in your MSW program regarding your current work that would have been helpful to you? I wish that the MSW would have had a stronger integration of leadership and management into social work values and clinical practice as a core part of the curriculum. I came into social work already being an entrepreneur, but not one that had focused on social outcomes necessarily. I learned a great deal about group dynamics and program evaluation in the MSW program and this has been very helpful. On the other hand, the history and

136 EFFECTIVENESS/PERFORMANCE MEASUREMENT

development of psychotherapy has little to do with running a business. It would have been great had more of the business pieces that I use on a daily basis in my work running a social purpose business been integrated into the teaching during my MSW program.

Chapter Summary

This chapter began with an introduction to the issues of impact, sustainability, and effectiveness/performance measurement and outlined the importance of these concepts in contemporary social work management. I then provided an overview of the various definitions of these concepts before discussing how each manifests itself in social work programs and organizations versus for-profit firms. A discussion of how to use logic models to guide the measurement process followed this. Finally, the chapter concluded with excerpts from an interview with a social work manager who leads a social purpose business. His reflections on impact, sustainability, and measurement were provided to illuminate some of the themes introduced earlier in the chapter.

The important concepts from this chapter to be sure to understand are as follows:

- Social impact is essentially defined as the degree to which a given human service program or organization meets the social mission or purpose it sets out to achieve. How well is the social problem being addressed?
- Financial performance or financial sustainability is a concept borrowed from the for-profit sector. This relates to a program or organization's ability to generate sufficient revenue to continue providing services into the future without interruption.
- Performance measurement in social work programs and organizations is inherently complicated. There is no "gold standard" measure or metric for measuring success. Combining social impact and financial sustainability, in the case of social enterprises, complicates matters further.
- A logic model is a useful tool in mapping out the social impact of a program or organization. It traces a service beneficiary (or

other input item, such as a volunteer or a staff member) from entry to ultimate exit from the program or organization. A logic model consists of the following categories: inputs, activities, outputs, and outcomes.

Suggested Learning Exercises

- How does the program where you work or do your field placement measure its performance? Does the program emphasize outputs, outcomes, some combination of both, or does it have some other emphasis for performance measurement? Does the program consider both impact and sustainability as it measures its performance? How would you explain your program's performance to a prospective funder? How could you enhance the way in which performance is measured in your program?
- Create a logic model for the program where you work or have your field placement. You may want to use Microsoft Word or PowerPoint to create the model. Remember to consider all inputs, activities, outputs, and outcomes for your program. If possible, in class, exchange logic models with a classmate and discuss the similarities and differences between them.
- A prospective funder for the program where you work or have your field placement wants to know how your program can achieve sustainability after her initial funding has run out (she intends to fund your program only for one year). Describe how you might achieve sustainability and decrease dependence on this particular funder's investment. Does your plan for sustainability affect the social impact dimension of your program? Explain how the social impact might be affected by the plan that you outline related to sustainability.

Internet Resources

Robin Hood Foundation—a recognized leader in measuring social impact, the foundation is based in New York City and funds many innovative projects in that geographical location. The website contains extensive information on the foundation's focus on metrics and the monetization of program outcomes: www.robinhood.org/metrics.

138   EFFECTIVENESS/PERFORMANCE MEASUREMENT

The Community Toolbox—a public service of the University of Kansas, which, among many useful resources, contains an in-depth discussion of logic models and how to create them (http://ctb.ku.edu/en/table contents/sub_section_main_1877.aspx). Other resources may be accessed from the homepage: http://ctb.ku.edu/en/default.aspx.

Social Impact Exchange—an intermediary organization that looks for impactful solutions to social problems and works to scale them up to effect change on a large scale. The group sponsors an annual conference, a business plan competition, and various webinars that are available for free on its website: www.socialimpactexchange.org.

PerformWell—a collaborative initiative of the Urban Institute, Child Trends, and Social Solutions, this website provides human services professionals with measurement tools for use in a variety of program settings: www.performwell.org.

Charting Impact—a strategic alliance among the BBB Wise Giving Alliance (www.bbb.org/us/Wise-Giving/), GuideStar (www.guidestar.org), and Independent Sector (www.independentsector.org), this initiative is designed to help social sector organizations understand and enhance their level of social impact in communities. The website also contains sample social impact reports, as well as Web-based resources on measuring the effectiveness and impact of your organization: www.chartingimpact.org/.

W. K. Kellogg Foundation—this well-known and large American philanthropic foundation publishes some useful resources in the knowledge center section of its website. The Logic Model Development Guide (www.wkkf.org/knowledge-center/resources/2006/02/wk-kellogg-foundation-logic-model-development-guide.aspx) and the Evaluation Handbook (www.wkkf.org/knowledge-center/resources/2010/w-k-kellogg-foundation-evaluation-handbook.aspx) are two examples. More here: www.wkkf.org/knowledge-center/knowledge-center-landing.aspx.

7

EMERGING ISSUES IN POLICY, ETHICS, AND NEW TECHNOLOGY

As introduced in the first chapter and elaborated upon throughout this book, the nature of social work management and the context in which social work managers operate is changing. Social work management is an evolving entrepreneurial and businesslike practice and, in recent years, has actually evolved quite rapidly in the United States and many other parts of the world. As with any practice that is developing in this manner, there are bound to be various gray areas or debated aspects of the practice that deserve attention. While my exploration in this chapter of some of social work management's emerging issues is by no means exhaustive, the issues I raise henceforth are not only important to consider, but also tend to be issues that are not often discussed in our field, at least not at sufficient length. Thus, this chapter serves as a forum to hopefully jump-start some new thinking on these topics.

The first part of this chapter will bring to your attention some of the issues that have recently emerged in the areas of organizational policy and practice ethics as social work managers and organizations become more businesslike, entrepreneurial, and so forth. Although I focus on the United States context in this commentary, much of what I describe can be applied to various other contexts. Finally, this chapter will briefly present some technological tools that are commonly utilized by contemporary social work managers. While this section of the chapter

140 EMERGING ISSUES

does not serve as a comprehensive guide to the use of technology in social work management and social entrepreneurship, I intend to provide a helpful introduction to some of the technologies commonly used and the benefits and/or detriments that the use of these technologies may introduce to a social work or human service organization.

An Unfavorable Business Climate Is Developing[1]

While embarking on your work as a social work management student or practitioner, it is important to keep in mind, as I have stressed throughout this book, that social work organizations are essentially businesses and must operate within a general business climate, which, unfortunately, seems to have become unfavorable in some respects. The Great Recession may have officially ended in June of 2009 according to the National Bureau of Economic Research, but for the most vulnerable among us—the homeless, jobless, hungry, disabled, and so forth— economic and emotional recovery is far from complete. Fortunately, most American communities are equipped with a variety of nonprofit human service organizations designed to assist individuals and families in need. But as demand for essential human services continues to increase in the wake of the deepest economic downturn in decades, many such organizations are struggling to maintain effectiveness.

Compounding these management challenges, it appears that some policymakers in the United States are further burdening the human service delivery system with misguided policies and regulations. It is my aim in this section of the chapter to critically examine a few recent developments in this regard and their potential impact on American nonprofit human service organizations—a major conduit for social work service provision.

First, the charitable tax deduction, a longtime incentive for philanthropic giving to charitable organizations (Schiller, 2012), has been in the crosshairs of President Obama and congressional members of both parties in recent months and years. Attempts to tinker with this giving incentive are nothing new, however (Germak, 2012). President Obama, with the implicit support of congressional Democrats, has attempted unsuccessfully in each of his budget proposals since he first took office in 2009 to cap the tax deductibility of charitable donations at 28 percent.

Put simply, this scenario would limit the financial incentive for charitable giving to 28 cents on the dollar; those in tax brackets higher than 28 percent would not receive increased financial benefits, as they currently receive, for gifts made to qualified charities.

While the "fiscal cliff" legislation of early 2013 and subsequent budget approvals have not included an outright cap or elimination of the charitable tax deduction as many in the nonprofit sector had feared, the "fiscal cliff" bill did introduce subtle constraints that could decelerate charitable giving in the coming years (Fleischer, 2013). Most notable is the "Pease provision" or personal exemption phase-out, often referred to as a "haircut" on itemized deductions (of all types) for higher-income earners, which, similar to an outright deduction cap, could serve as a disincentive for wealthy Americans seeking to donate substantial amounts of money to charity (Donovan, 2013).

This is a mistake. Capping, eliminating, or otherwise toying with the tax deductibility of charitable donations will hurt nonprofit human service organizations, especially smaller, grassroots-type agencies, many of which rely heavily on charitable donations. If we must, as some policymakers desire to do, adjust the charitable deduction to raise more revenue (or for other political or ideological reasons), I suggest we do so only for gifts to nonprofit organizations—museums, arts organizations, and the like—that do not directly serve our most vulnerable. This notion of a "carve-out" for the human services will not be popular among many in the nonprofit sector, but we should prioritize what is the most prudent and important use of constrained resources.

In addition to the charitable tax deduction debate, other policy and regulatory trends have recently emerged that, over time, could negatively affect the nonprofit human service sector. First, some states, including those with many human service nonprofits such as New Jersey and New York, have begun cracking down on what they view as runaway compensation packages for nonprofit leaders and other apparently frivolous spending by contracted nonprofit organizations. Salary caps are now becoming common in state contracts, as are limits on fringe benefits for executives and managers, as well as constraints on professional development expenditures for all employees. To be sure, restrictions of this nature typically only pertain to public funds; at least in theory an organization can do what it wants with non-public or non-government funds. Still, this creates an odd dichotomy of working capital with which organizations must operate, which is a constraint unlike that experienced by most corporations.

Admittedly, no one believes that nonprofit leaders should receive unreasonable compensation or that nonprofit employee perks should be lavish, but, according to Pallotta (2008), it is also true that a competitive talent market exists and organizations get what they pay for. Leadership of multimillion-dollar operations, in the case of some midsized nonprofit organizations, requires specialized skill and should be paid for accordingly. Compensation caps and professional development restrictions could, going forward, limit the ability of human service nonprofits to attract and retain top talent, affect organizational performance, and ultimately have a negative impact on service beneficiaries.

Finally, despite all of the significant benefits to vulnerable populations of recent healthcare reform, the new legislation passed in 2010 could present some organizational management challenges. Namely, beginning in 2015 (the Obama administration recently postponed this by one year from 2014 to 2015), nonprofit human service organizations with 50 or more full-time employees will need to grapple with the employer mandates of the Patient Protection and Affordable Care Act (PPACA), which will require organizations of all types with 50 or more full-time employees to provide affordable health insurance coverage to all employees and their dependents, or pay substantial penalties. As a result, nonprofit human service organizations may need to contribute more to employee and dependent healthcare premiums in order to make employer-sponsored insurance affordable as required by law. However, many human service nonprofits currently do not contribute anything toward an employee's dependent coverage because it is cost-prohibitive to do so. New mandates included in the PPACA could prove quite costly if human service organizations must begin to increase premium contributions to meet affordability requirements.

While some midsized for-profit businesses may lay off employees, cut work hours, or utilize consultants to stay below the threshold of 50 full-time employees, human service nonprofits cannot easily do that, nor should they, due to the essential nature of most direct service employees. Additionally, some employers may choose to pay penalties instead of offering health insurance benefits, but it would be unthinkable for human service organizations to drop coverage for employees, many of whom have dedicated their careers to working with vulnerable populations for modest pay. Thus, it seems to me that human service nonprofits should be exempted, if possible, from the PPACA's employer mandates.

In summary, I am concerned about what appears to be an unfavorable business climate for nonprofit human service organizations that is developing in the United States. Specifically, changes in tax deductibility for charitable donations, compensation and employee benefit restrictions, and employer mandates in healthcare reform are a few policy and regulatory issues that, combined, could significantly squeeze human service nonprofit organizations in the near future. Now is not the time to burden these organizations with such policies and regulations. To the extent possible, government should take a step back and let nonprofit human service organizations serve those in need as they have been doing for some time.

Ethical Considerations for Social Entrepreneurship and Businesslike Social Work Management[2]

In addition to the above issues regarding policy and regulatory concerns, social work managers desiring to become full-fledged social entrepreneurs must pay attention to ethical considerations affecting their practice. Social work is a profession governed by ethics and values; therefore, any social worker practicing social entrepreneurship must abide by the Code of Ethics of the National Association of Social Workers (NASW, 1999). The ethical dilemmas initially encountered by the practice of social entrepreneurship involve the following ethical standards as presented in the NASW Code of Ethics (NASW, 1999): (1) commitment to clients; and (2) payment for services. Indeed, as the field of social entrepreneurship grows and more social workers partake in enterprising activities, more ethical dilemmas will most definitely arise and need to be resolved.

First, according to the NASW Code of Ethics (NASW, 1999), a client's interests must be of primary concern to a social worker. However,

144 EMERGING ISSUES

social work managers need to respond to many stakeholders in addition to clients such as funding sources, government regulatory agencies, the media, and so forth. According to Gummer (1997), the NASW Code of Ethics, in its ethical standard involving commitment to clients, focuses incompletely on relations between practitioner and client. Gummer explains, "The notion that the social agency is responsible primarily to clients is both unrealistic and undesirable" (p. 143).

Given the complexity of social work management, especially in this era of evolving businesslike practice, social work entrepreneurs must make a sincere effort to balance their commitments to clients and to external stakeholders simultaneously. If a social work manager leading a substance use treatment program, for example, were to lose focus on the market demand for services and improperly forecast future revenues, the clients would perhaps be well served in the short term, but the enterprise would probably need to be shut down in the long term due to inadequate fiscal foresight on the part of the executive—an ethical impropriety of enormous scale. In essence, social workers practicing social entrepreneurship will continuously face an ethical dilemma regarding commitment to clients: there is no way to avoid a social work manager's responsibilities to the myriad of stakeholders in both the internal and external environments. To address this dilemma in social enterprises and entrepreneurial social work organizations, it would be prudent to establish a committee to periodically review the social entrepreneur's adherence to his or her commitment to clients because without such commitment, albeit a balanced one, the entrepreneur loses sight of the *social* aspect of social entrepreneurship.

In addition to commitment to clients, payment for services is a second ethical dilemma encountered by social workers involved in social entrepreneurship. On the one hand, Masi (1992) suggests that there is no good reason why social workers cannot work in for-profit, proprietary settings or behave entrepreneurially, compensating themselves accordingly for innovative practice. In fact, other helping professionals such as physicians typically do not have qualms about charging market-rate fees to patients with the ability to pay. Such professionals are usually compensated accordingly. Likewise, social workers should not necessarily take a vow of poverty even though they frequently work with populations stricken by poverty. Arguably, a for-profit mentality, such as higher compensation levels for social workers or bonus schemes, could attract more talent to the field and bolster the morale of those already practicing at marginally acceptable income levels (Giffords, 2000; Guo, 2006). On the other hand, Egan and Kadushin (1999) and Kurzman (1976) rightly assert that social workers not only have the responsibility to serve clients who can pay for services, but also to accommodate those clients perhaps so marginalized that they may not have any health insurance coverage, let alone money, to pay for social work services. Further, as the NASW (1998) adeptly argues, social workers must never let the desire for increased compensation steer their judgment concerning which clients to serve.

Essentially, social workers must treat all clients fairly. For example, if social workers in a hospital setting receive a monetary bonus for treating clients with third-party insurance, these social workers cannot discriminate against clients with Medicaid, for instance. Froelich (1999) describes such a discriminatory practice as *creaming*, which can have longstanding negative effects on the well-being of the client population. A solution to such a predicament would be to set aside ample time to see Medicaid-insured clients each day, regardless of how many *profitable* clients may be present. In a sense, this would be an affirmative action type of policy for social work. Such a mentality will be increasingly important as social workers embark on social entrepreneurship initiatives, and entrepreneurial managers will face the imperative to instill such values in their employees.

It is important to recognize that as a social worker bound by the NASW Code of Ethics, one must advocate for clients for whom no one else advocates. If one is organized at work, there will be many opportunities to work with clients tied to increased compensation and, in addition, with clients who do not have the ability to pay. Ultimately, administrators must strive to balance commitments to clients with commitments to external stakeholders, including funding sources. This creates an additional ethical task for entrepreneurial social workers. According to Kurzman (2000), social workers operating in industries outside of traditional social work

146 EMERGING ISSUES

must not only abide by the NASW Code of Ethics, but also establish a "normative discipline of morality that underscores the principles of advocacy and equity" (p. 160).

One final note regarding ethics: it is imperative that social work managers maintain a practical perspective regarding ethical dilemmas and the reality of their agencies' external environments. As Ayers, Mindel, Robinson, and Wright (1981) point out, after all ethical dilemmas have been considered, human service leaders must view fees for service as essential to the survival of their agencies. This study was published in 1981. It would be a tremendous understatement to imply that earned income, such as client fees, is more essential today to the financial sustainability of social service agencies when, in fact, the practice of charging client fees has been a commonly accepted practice for over three decades.

New Technology and the Human Services

In this final section of this chapter related to emerging issues in social work management, I will explore issues related to the following "new" technologies that are increasingly being utilized in human service organizations: e-mail, social media, and mobile devices and apps. These emerging technologies present both great opportunities for enhancing the work of human service programs and organizations while, at the same time, posing some challenges to social work managers with regard to appropriate oversight and management of their usage.

One caveat I should mention before proceeding: I realize that these examples may not be extremely new technologies. Electronic mail, for instance, has existed and been used by human service organizations for more than a decade. Still, e-mail continues to be a technology that needs close monitoring and strategic direction in order to be an effective tool for social work service delivery. Moreover, there has not been much attention paid to the use of e-mail in social work management books. For these reasons, I introduce this topic here. Furthermore, the following is a brief introduction to these tools and is by no means exhaustive. Entire books could be written on the management of each of these technologies, and there are plenty of other technological tools that social work managers might choose to adopt, some of which are extremely

EMERGING ISSUES   147

new and do not yet have a track record from which to derive meaningful discussion. Nonetheless, based on my practice experience, the following tools are worthy of some discussion given that they are being used frequently and widely by social workers at all levels within human service organizations.

E-Mail

For some of you reading this book, you may not even remember what the world was like before the advent of e-mail. In the late 1990s, e-mail use began to flourish in both personal and business settings. Human service organizations began to adopt e-mail systems around this time to enhance communication among staff. E-mail began to play an increasingly important role in community outreach, fundraising, and so forth. While it may seem rather mundane to discuss e-mail as a new technology in a book released during this current decade, I would argue that e-mail still deserves attention. After all, I only started using e-mail in my work as a social worker in 2004 when I was issued my first work-related e-mail account at the human service organization where I worked.

So, what have we learned about e-mail use by social workers in the human services over the past 10 years approximately? First, e-mail has greatly reduced the time needed to communicate about business issues, including things such as client referrals, staff communications, and the like. However, it is very important to realize that most e-mail systems, especially those used by many human service organizations, are not secure environments for transmitting data. It is now quite the norm in some agencies, for instance, to send client referral information as attachments to e-mail messages. Realize, however, that when client information is transmitted via e-mail, there is always a risk that it might be viewed by unintended recipients. The same holds true for sensitive information about staff members that is sent via e-mail.

While I am not at all arguing for the elimination of e-mail use in the human services, I do think it is incumbent upon social work managers to develop appropriate oversight of its use. Such oversight could take the form of developing policies for the use of e-mail in human service agencies, for example. It is highly recommended that human service programs and organizations have policies that guide staff members through the use of e-mail for client-related matters and other work-related reasons. A policy not only helps to guide workers, but also provides management with an accountability mechanism. A social worker who inappropriately uses an agency e-mail system could be held accountable, disciplined, or even terminated from employment depending on the situation. It is very difficult to take such measures as a social work manager without such a policy in place.

One final thing I would like to mention about e-mail has to do with the strategic use of e-mail by social work managers. Assuming that we, as social work managers, follow all policies and use e-mail appropriately and cautiously, there are still ways in which we can leverage e-mail to enhance our management practice. For example, it has always been a practice of mine to not let e-mail messages in my inbox linger for too long without sending a reply. People that send us e-mail messages, especially our supervisees, expect and want to receive replies from us. I completely understand that it is frequently challenging to deal with the volume of incoming e-mail, especially as the program or organization you oversee becomes larger and more complex. Still, it is good practice to try to respond in a timely manner to all incoming messages. Your responses can be relatively short and, in some instances, you may just need to acknowledge that you have received an e-mail and that a more elaborate reply will be forthcoming. This type of behavior will go a long way in satisfying your staff members or others that send you e-mail messages. By replying in a timely manner, you will build a reputation for being responsive and attuned to people's needs. I usually make sure to clear my inbox (i.e. reply to all received messages in a given day) by the end of the evening on the day the e-mails were received; I do not usually let an e-mail message linger for more than one day. This type of strategic e-mail management should help you become more effective in your daily work as a social work manager.

Social Media

Like e-mail, social media use has risen in recent years both for personal reasons and also for work-related reasons in human service organization environments. LinkedIn, Facebook, Twitter, and many other social media services have become a part of daily life for many social workers and human service organizations. There are both challenges and opportunities associated with the rise in social media usage similar to those associated with e-mail usage. First, social media is an even less secure environment for data transmission than e-mail is. A social media platform such as Facebook is extremely public, and what gets posted there can find its way in many directions, most unknown to the person or organization that originally posted the information. This raises obvious ethical issues for human service organizations that wish to use social media for client outreach and communications.

Whether social media is allowed in the workplace is a decision that each individual human service organization must make depending on a variety of factors, such as the client population served, the benefits versus the risks of social media usage, and so on. As with e-mail, much of this dilemma can be minimized with the introduction of strong social media policies with which staff members must abide. Social media policies that both guide social work staff and provide for accountability mechanisms are an extremely good idea for the social work manager to implement. The challenge is often deciding where to draw the lines around the appropriate use of social media, which really depends on the nature of the work performed by a particular program or organization.

Despite these potential risks, social media can provide considerable opportunities for social work managers that understand how to appropriately use social media tools and oversee their use by social work staff. Fundraising, for example, can be enhanced by using social media. As a social work manager, you could post various success stories (you must always first obtain consent from clients to use their names and likenesses) on your LinkedIn profile, for example. These stories can then be "liked" and shared by others in your professional network. If you are connected with funders or other decision-makers via LinkedIn, your good news will immediately be in front of them. I can attest from personal experience that such a practice can lead to very positive outcomes for social work programs and organizations.

The key thing to remember about social media use is that it can deliver your message to a very wide audience. People in this audience, some of whom you may not even know yet, could possibly be helpful to you and your organization. If you choose not to use social media in this manner,

150 EMERGING ISSUES

you are essentially reducing your sphere of influence as a social work manager, which could lead to your human service program or organization being outcompeted for funding, client referrals, staff recruitment, and so forth.

Mobile Devices and Apps

At what seems like a rapid pace, mobile technologies are being adopted and put to use by all of us and changing the way we operate in our personal lives and also in the workplace. Smartphones and tablets, for instance, have become ubiquitous in many contexts. It is difficult to find a professional social worker these days, especially those just starting their careers, that is not using a mobile device for personal matters. Many social workers are also using their devices for business purposes. Social work managers need to know that people do not leave their devices at home when they show up to work; it is nearly impossible to ban the use of mobile devices at work. Devices such as iPhones, iPads, and the like are being used in the workplace whether organizations plan for this or not. As with e-mail and social media, the main dilemma for the social work manager becomes how to harness these technologies and provide for their appropriate and effective usage in a human service organization.

My philosophy as a social work manager when it comes to the use of mobile devices has always been to accept the fact that my staff members are using their devices anyway and to allow them to do so while also asking them to follow the appropriate protocol for using their devices in the workplace. As with all new technology, I think that developing a policy for social work staff is very beneficial. Most human service organizations do not have a mobile device policy, but I argue that such a policy will help to clarify for staff members what they can and cannot do at work with regard to their mobile devices.

Social work managers also need to consider whether to issue smartphones, for example, to social work staff or to ask staff to use their own devices. This latter scenario has recently been described as a bring-your-own-device (BYOD) approach, which could be a good way for smaller human service organizations with constrained budgets to encourage responsible mobile usage at work. However, in this scenario, organizations need to compensate employees in some way for using a personal device for work-related matters. This could occur by way of the organization paying for a portion of the monthly mobile bill for each staff, or by some other method of compensation that is agreeable to staff members and makes fiscal sense for the organization. Despite what might seem like challenging implementation details, it is often more cost-effective to use BYOD than to purchase new mobile equipment and service plans for all social work staff in a program or organization. Each setting is different, however, and how you approach the mobile technology issue will depend on the unique needs of your program or organization.

Finally, it should be noted that there are many emerging opportunities for social work as a field to embrace the use of mobile applications or "apps." Assuming, as described above, that social work staff members are already using mobile devices for personal and work matters, we should encourage more application development and usage in the social work field. The main purpose of using an app as opposed to a more traditional method of working is that an app can help to organize commonly performed processes on a convenient mobile device. In the field of social work, apps are not as commonly used as they may be in other fields, such as medicine, nursing, or even banking, as examples. However, the day will probably soon come when social work case managers, for instance, are performing their job duties on their smartphones by way of a mobile app. Case records and notes, referrals, intake processes, and so forth could soon all be performed in one place via a mobile app rather than through disparate management systems. Indeed, case managers could perform these necessary tasks while visiting clients in the field, which would save both time and money for an organization. In short, there are exciting possibilities emerging in this area. Social work managers should be ready for this next wave of new technology, which will need to be appropriately leveraged and managed, similar to e-mail and social media, once it is commonplace.

Chapter Summary

This chapter served as an introduction to a select variety of emerging issues facing the field of social work management, but was not an exhaustive list of issues facing the field. The chapter began by exploring a few policy and regulatory issues that are creating a somewhat unfavorable business climate in which human service organizations must operate in the United States. Next, ethical issues were introduced that are facing social work managers working in businesslike or entrepreneurial settings. Finally, a few select emerging technologies used by social work managers and human service organizations were introduced and the challenges and opportunities of each were explored.

The important concepts from this chapter to be sure to understand are as follows:

- There are a few important policy and regulatory issues that are emerging and deserving of attention in the human service industry in the United States: the tax deductibility of charitable contributions to nonprofit human service organizations, compensation levels for social work managers and leaders, and organizational effects of recent healthcare reform legislation.
- Two areas of ethical concerns, as per the NASW Code of Ethics, facing social work managers that behave in a businesslike or entrepreneurial manner are: (1) commitment to clients; and (2) payment for services. Contemporary social work managers should pay special attention to these areas of ethical concern.
- Among the many emerging technologies available to social work managers and human service organizations, e-mail, social media, and mobile devices and apps are important to understand both because of the challenges they present for programs and organizations and the opportunities that can be leveraged for more effective work performance.

Suggested Learning Exercises

- Try to arrange a brief meeting with the executive director or chief executive officer at your place of employment or at your field placement. Ask this person his or her thoughts on the "employer mandate" of the PPACA that is scheduled to take effect in 2015. What changes, if any, does the organization plan to make with regard to health insurance coverage for employees? How will the organization handle family coverage? Spousal or domestic partner coverage? If possible, compare the notes from your interview with others in your class. There will inevitably be differences in responses from the executives—why do you think this is the case?

- Examine the NASW Code of Ethics in its entirety (www.social workers.org/pubs/code/default.asp). Identify every area that you think could raise potential ethical issues if you were to launch a social enterprise (or were to operate a program or organization from a truly businesslike perspective). Suggest changes to the Code of Ethics that might help to incorporate the practice of social entrepreneurship or businesslike social work management.
- Ask your supervisor at work or where you do your field placement for a copy of the organization's social media policy. If one exists and you are able to obtain a copy of it, analyze this policy by answering the following questions. What is the underlying objective of the policy? How effective is this policy in achieving this objective? What changes would you suggest be made to the policy? If a policy does not exist (or you are not able to obtain one), compose a draft social media policy for the organization. Ask to see a copy of a different agency policy so that you can base your social media policy on the same template.

Internet Resources

Independent Sector—a national policy advocacy organization for nonprofits based in Washington, DC. The organization represents the interests of over 600 member nonprofit organizations on a national level and also hosts an annual capacity-building conference. The website includes timely policy briefs and white papers related to broad nonprofit issues—both emerging and longstanding ones: www.independent sector.org.

National Council of Nonprofits—an aggregate network of state nonprofit associations that seeks to coordinate and mobilize nonprofits to achieve collective impact. The website contains important and timely information on state and local policy issues affecting nonprofits: www.councilof nonprofits.org.

Charity Defense Council—a new organization started by nonprofit activist and author Dan Pallotta, which aims to defend nonprofit organizations against policy developments, such as executive compensation caps, that portend to hamper the social impact of human service organizations: http://charitydefensecouncil.org.

Techsoup.org—a nonprofit intermediary organization committed to connecting nonprofit organizations with effective technology products and innovative solutions. The website contains options for purchasing discounted technology products, as well as a vibrant community forum with blogs and other resource articles: www.techsoup.org.

Nonprofit Technology Network (NTEN)—a membership organization of nonprofit professionals who use technology to achieve their social missions. The website contains a wide array of free resources and learning tools: www.nten.org.

National Association of Social Workers (NASW) Code of Ethics—this is probably not the first time you have studied this document, but social work managers operating at a macro level must also adhere to the principles and standards contained herein: www.socialworkers.org/pubs/code/code.asp.

Nonprofit Law Blog—an active blog site with postings on a variety of important topics, including emerging issues, such as employment law changes, charitable giving policy developments, and mergers and acquisitions within the nonprofit sector: www.nonprofitlawblog.com.

Notes

1. This section contains material from Germak's 2013 "Guest editorial note," *Administration in Social Work*, 37(2), 103–105, reprinted by permission of the publisher.
2. This section contains material from Germak and Singh's 2010 article, "Social entrepreneurship: Changing the way social workers do business," *Administration in Social Work*, 34(1): 79–95, reprinted by permission of the publisher.

8
CONCLUSION

Congratulations—you have reached the end of this book and are well on your way to enhancing your skills as a social work management student or practitioner. At this point, I encourage you to review what you have learned and seek to apply some of the concepts by doing the following. First, in the following section, I have included the key points from each chapter in one convenient location for your review. If there are any points that continue to be unclear, you may want to revisit the chapter in which that key point was discussed for further exploration. In addition, I encourage you to work through the suggested learning exercises at the end of each chapter if you have not done so already. These have been designed to specifically test your knowledge on some of the most important concepts introduced in this book. Finally, there is a case profile, including discussion questions and a full business plan included as an appendix to this book. Exploring this case would be a good way to apply many of the concepts presented in this book. Now, let us quickly review the book's key points.

Review of Key Points from All Chapters

Chapter 1 served as an introduction to the emerging practice of business-like social work management and social entrepreneurship. The chapter introduced the following key points:

156 CONCLUSION

- Social work management has evolved in recent years to become more businesslike and entrepreneurial.
- Social entrepreneurship—a term used broadly to refer to businesslike social work management practice—is a growing phenomenon that combines business management skills with social work practice. Social enterprise, social venturing, social innovation, and so forth are similar concepts.
- Becoming businesslike is not easy for most social workers, but essential business skills can be learned during a degree program or afterward.
- Businesslike social work managers can find meaningful employment in an array of organizational types: nonprofit, for-profit, hybrid, and others.
- The essential social work management business skill domains, which complement social work skill domains, are: financial management, talent management, and the management of marketing, sales, and communications.

In Chapter 2, financial management was explored and the following key points were introduced:

- Proper financial oversight and management can ensure that clients of human service programs and organizations receive adequate and necessary services.
- The accounting equation used in nonprofit organizations is: Assets = Liabilities + Net Assets.
- The balance sheet, income statement, and statement of cash flows are the three standardized financial statements used in nonprofit human service programs. Social work managers should be comfortable analyzing and interpreting all of these statements.
- Projecting revenue and expense is a key skill, however there is always uncertainty involved with making projections.
- Nonprofit human service organizations have a distinct capital structure from that of for-profit firms, although the nature and mix of this capital structure is evolving.

Chapter 3 introduced the concept of talent management, an essential component of social work management, and included the following key points:

- The human resources or personnel of a social work organization should be viewed as talent and the process of managing these resources should be referred to as talent management.
- Talent management and financial management must be balanced in social work organizations due to frequently constrained resources and trade-offs that social work managers must make.
- Social work is truly a service business in which the relationship between client and social worker is a key driver of a program's success.
- Effective talent management involves a social work manager knowing how to manage in all directions: downward, upward, and sideways.

Chapter 4 served as an introduction to marketing, sales, and communications skills. The chapter's key points are as follows:

- Marketing is more than just advertising—it is a process that involves everything necessary to bring a given product or service to market.
- The most common marketing frameworks are the Four P's (product, price, place, and promotion) and STP (segment-target-position).
- Selling is a distinct function from marketing, but the two processes are highly related.
- The sales process involves selling to both internal (within your organization) and external (outside of your organization) constituents.
- Communications processes are highly correlated to both marketing and selling, and there are various communications tactics that can help the social work manager to be successful in marketing and selling.

In Chapter 5, business planning was introduced as an effective and necessary process in contemporary human service organizations. The following key points were presented in this chapter:

- Business planning, once only a process known to for-profit organizations, is becoming commonplace in human service organizations and, in fact, social work managers are being asked by funders to create business plans for programs and organizations as opposed to more traditional applications for grant funding.
- The main difference between a social work-type business plan and a commercial business plan is that the former focuses on not only financial viability, but also social impact—the degree to which the social problems addressed are resolved.
- A business plan for a social work program or organization should be approximately 30 pages in length and include the following eight components (refer to Appendix 3 of this book for a sample business plan): (1) executive summary; (2) program concept; (3) market and competition analysis; (4) marketing plan; (5) operations plan; (6) financial plan; (7) management team info; and (8) appendices.

Chapter 6 included a discussion of the definitions of impact and sustainability, and the methods by which each of these important concepts can be measured. These are the key points discussed in this chapter:

- Social impact is essentially defined as the degree to which a given human service program or organization meets the social mission or purpose it sets out to achieve. How well is the social problem being addressed?
- Financial performance or financial sustainability is a concept borrowed from the for-profit sector. This relates to a program or organization's ability to generate sufficient revenue to continue providing services into the future without interruption.

- Performance measurement in social work programs and organizations is inherently complicated. There is no "gold standard" measure or metric for measuring success. Combining social impact and financial sustainability, in the case of social enterprises, complicates matters further.
- A logic model is a useful tool in mapping out the social impact of a program or organization. It traces a service beneficiary (or other input item, such as a volunteer or a staff member) from entry to ultimate exit from the program or organization. A logic model consists of the following categories: inputs, activities, outputs, and outcomes.

Finally, Chapter 7 provided an overview of some of the emerging issues facing social work managers and human service organizations. The following key points were discussed:

- There are a few important policy and regulatory issues that are emerging and deserving of attention in the human service industry in the United States: the tax deductibility of charitable contributions to nonprofit human service organizations, compensation levels for social work managers and leaders, and organizational effects of recent healthcare reform legislation.
- Two areas of ethical concerns, as per the NASW Code of Ethics, facing social work managers that behave in a businesslike or entrepreneurial manner are: (1) commitment to clients; and (2) payment for services. Contemporary social work managers should pay special attention to these areas of ethical concern.
- Among the many emerging technologies available to social work managers and human service organizations, e-mail, social media, and mobile devices and apps are important to understand both because of the challenges they present for programs and organizations and the opportunities that can be leveraged for more effective work performance.

Closing Remarks

It has given me great pleasure to write this book and share these business skills with you. Much of what is in this book I have found to be quite helpful in my social work career thus far. I have discussed these issues with students in the social work courses that I teach (even though these topics are not usually part of the official syllabi), as well as with staff that I have supervised through the years. Now these teaching opportunities are more widely available in book format, and for this I am grateful and excited at the possibility of sharing this knowledge with a wide audience.

My sincere hope is that you can use the lessons included in this book to complement what you are learning in your social work program if you are a student. If you are a practicing social work manager, I trust that some of these lessons will augment your current skill set in order to optimize your effectiveness in your work. Either way, it is essential that contemporary social work managers be equipped with the most inclusive skill set possible.

This book includes a good deal of information and key points, as outlined above. However, as my closing thought, I would like to reiterate that the foundation of this book rests on a few key areas: (1) financial management; (2) talent management; and (3) marketing, sales, and communications. These are important skill areas for social work management that are not frequently taught in social work degree programs, if at all. Time and time again, I have witnessed practicing social work managers (including myself!) that need these skills but have not received proper training in these areas. Therefore, use this book as a steppingstone to further skill development. If a particular area, such as financial management, continues to be a challenge for you, try to enroll in a continuing education course or pick up another book that is solely dedicated to that topic. Having read this book and understood its contents, you should now have a solid foundation in the business skills essential to social work management. I wish you the best of luck and great success in your work as a social work manager.

APPENDIX 1
PARENT UNIVERSE

PROFILE OF A SOCIAL ENTERPRISE FOUNDED BY A SOCIAL WORKER

The following is a brief profile of a social enterprise, Parent Universe, founded by a social work manager soon after receiving her MSW degree. This brief profile, combined with the full business plan that follows, is intended to provide a practical overview of the concept of social entrepreneurship and business planning within a social work context. Discussion questions are also included to facilitate further learning in this area.

A Social Enterprise Emerges

Parent Universe officially launched in May 2013, although the idea for the social venture was first conceived during an MSW class and further refined when a team from PCANJ, led by recent MSW graduate Patty Mojta, applied in October 2011 to the New Jersey Social Innovation Institute, a training program for nascent social entrepreneurs. This training institute ran from January through July of 2012, which is when the team at PCANJ formalized the social enterprise idea into a business plan. Ms. Mojta hired and trained her first part-time consultant employee in May 2013 and the enterprise was then open and ready for business. Initial seed funding of $2,500 soon followed from the PCANJ board of directors. The social enterprise thus became fully operational at the start of the 2013–2014 fiscal year, July 1, 2013.

Parent Universe is an earned-income social enterprise that is wholly controlled and operated by Prevent Child Abuse New Jersey (PCANJ), a tax-exempt, charitable organization headquartered in New Brunswick, NJ. PCANJ is exempt from paying tax on its income in accordance with section 501(c)3 of the U.S. Tax Code. Parent Universe is structured as a mission-related unit of the parent organization and, as such, is also exempt from paying tax on its income. Parent Universe does not have an independent legal structure.

Currently, Parent Universe is led by its founder, Patty Mojta, who is an MSW-level licensed social work manager at PCANJ. She reports directly to the vice president of PCANJ, who reports to the executive director. Ms. Mojta makes the day-to-day decisions about operations, budgeting/spending, marketing, etc. for Parent Universe.

Supporting the Overall Mission through Social Entrepreneurship

PCANJ is trying to solve the problem of child abuse and neglect through prevention programs. Prevention programs largely include education and support for parents during the early stages of parenting before child abuse can occur.

Parent Universe, as a social enterprise subsidiary of PCANJ, supports this overall agency mission. The mission of Parent Universe is to support new parents during the exciting time surrounding the birth of a baby. According to Ms. Mojta:

> We know from research that home visitation programs lead to better outcomes for children in terms of mental health, physical health, school performance, adult earning potential, and much more. Parents who invest in their children early on will see a value in terms of increased lifelong health and well-being.

Parent Universe provides a variety of home-based supportive services to families during pregnancy and throughout the first three years of a child's life. Parent Universe's signature service, Baby Coaching, includes

APPENDIX 1   163

customized one-on-one sessions with a parenting and child development expert to assist parents with encouraging optimal growth and development of a child. In addition to Baby Coaching, Parent Universe offers prenatal education packages on topics such as childbirth education, breastfeeding education, and infant care and safety. Parent Universe also holds workshops in the community on topics that are important to new and expectant parents.

A Focus on Social Impact and Financial Sustainability

While the target market for Parent Universe includes primarily upper-income and middle-income families, it is building a structure to ultimately be able to reach clients across all income brackets. All services are offered for a fee and are à la carte. Thus, at least in theory, families on nearly any budget can access the help they need. The general plan is to use the revenue generated from paying customers to be able to offer free supportive services to parents who cannot afford to pay. Additionally, Parent Universe has developed employee benefit packages in an attempt to reach parents in any income bracket (high, middle, low) through offering the services via an employer's benefits package.

The indicators used to determine the social impact of Parent Universe are measured at the individual level. In terms of individual customers, the enterprise has a survey that measures parents' sense of competence, knowledge of parenting and child development, and nurturing and attachment—all protective factors against child abuse and neglect. From a social return on investment standpoint, Ms. Mojta believes that preventing child abuse effectively reduces the likelihood of so many problems throughout a person's life—mental illness, substance abuse, criminal activity, poor school performance, and the likelihood of the child becoming an adult who his or her children.

As for financial sustainability, Ms. Mojta explains, "We project that when we scale to a tipping point of 4,000 coaching sessions per year, we can generate significant revenue to help support our parent agency [PCANJ] as well as sustain Parent Universe." She adds that when the enterprise gets to this scale, the goal will be to reach thousands of beneficiaries. The reason for striving for high numbers of service beneficiaries, according to Ms. Mojta, is to achieve greater social *and* financial impact. Serving such large numbers of beneficiaries would indeed provide social impact and also bring much needed revenue to the enterprise and to the parent organization.

Key Success Factors and Challenges in Launching a Social Enterprise

According to Ms. Mojta, a key success factor related to launching a social enterprise within a larger nonprofit human service organization is the presence of a positive organizational culture that supports creativity, innovation, and professional development. This positive culture at her organization has helped her to navigate the many complications inherent to a launch of a new business venture. She also feels that a great organizational strength that can be leveraged is staff expertise. In her case, this has been organizational expertise in parenting and child development, program development, program evaluation, and nationally recognized evidence-based child abuse prevention programs.

A few challenges related to social entrepreneurship in the context of a larger parent agency, at least during the start-up phase of the venture, are lack of staff time and lack of sufficient resources (Ms. Mojta, at this point, is essentially working two full-time jobs as founding director of the social enterprise and another full-time job at the parent organization). Moreover, there is a general lack of experience with business management and fee-based ventures at all levels of many human service organizations, including at PCANJ, which makes launching and sustaining a social enterprise quite challenging.

APPENDIX 2
PARENT UNIVERSE
DISCUSSION QUESTIONS

Based on this brief profile and the full business plan for Parent Universe that follows this profile, the following questions are provided for class discussion and/or independent study:

1. What are the key distinguishing features that separate Parent Universe from a traditional social work program or service (e.g. your field placement program or the program where you work)? How do you envision Parent Universe to look and feel different from a more traditional social work program? How do you feel about the nature of this program? Do you have reactions either for or against this type of program?

2. What are some of the potential ethical issues related to the growth and expansion of this social enterprise? How might you mitigate these ethical issues? Refer to the NASW Code of Ethics (1999) as you consider this question.

3. Parent Universe seeks to achieve significant scale (i.e. becoming a very large provider of services). What challenges do you anticipate Parent Universe will encounter as it scales up its services? How would you address these challenges? What do you think about scaling up versus staying small (refer to the interview with Wendell Knight in Chapter 6)?

4. How prepared would you be for developing a social enterprise of this nature? What would your strengths be? Where would you be weak? What do you think that Patty Mojta needed to learn in addition to what she learned during her MSW program? How does one acquire these additional skills?
5. Do you think that social entrepreneurship, as described in this case profile, is a worthwhile endeavor? Why or why not? Ultimately, how do we know whether social entrepreneurship is an effective social work intervention? Conversely, how do we know whether more traditional interventions are effective?

APPENDIX 3
PARENT UNIVERSE

A PLACE FOR PARENTS WHO THINK THE WORLD OF THEIR CHILDREN

BUSINESS PLAN

TABLE OF CONTENTS

Business Plan Summary
Parent Universe Business Model
Market Demand and Opportunity
Social Impact

Description of the Enterprise
Our Services
Our Innovative Approach
Key Innovations
Theory of Change
Mission Statement
Core Values
Goals and Measurement
Social Return on Investment
Competitive Advantage
Inaction

The Team and Organizational Background
The Team
About Prevent Child Abuse New Jersey
Legal Structure
Current Status
Advisors

The Market and Industry
Industry Description and Market Segments
Target Market Segments
Expected Position in Target Market Segments

Marketing Plan
Fundraising Targets and Strategies
Products and Pricing Plan
Placement and Promotion

APPENDIX 3   169

The Financial Plan

Operations Plan
Definition of Success
Intermediate Goals and Success Measures
Timeline

Risk Assessment
Financial Risk
Legal Risk
Talent Risk
Environmental Risk

Supporting Documents
Appendix A: Child Abuse in the US*
Appendix B: Organizational Chart of Parent Universe
Appendix C: Logic Model*
Appendix D: Survey of Birth Professionals
Appendix E: Customer Survey
Appendix F: Resume of Social Entrepreneur
Appendix G: Marketing Plan
Appendix H: Corporate Proposal
Appendix I: Year 1 Income Statement
Appendix J: 5-Year Income Statement*
References

---

* These appendices are included in this book. All other appendices are available from
the book's author upon request.

BUSINESS PLAN SUMMARY

Parent Universe is a social venture that provides parent education and support services to new or expecting parents with children ages 0–3 in New Jersey. Parent Universe is designed to be self-sustaining through earned income. By Year 2, we project that we will generate additional revenue to support the operating costs of our parent nonprofit organization, Prevent Child Abuse New Jersey, as well as expand the availability of parent support services to a low-income population. The proceeds generated from this venture will enhance the services of Prevent Child Abuse New Jersey.

Parent Universe Business Model

Our signature service, Baby Coaching, consists of customized one-on-one sessions to assist parents with encouraging optimal growth and development of their child. Baby Coaches are certified Parent Educators who:

- Meet with parents in the convenience of their own home.
- Provide **educational sessions** tailored to the family's wishes.
- Have expertise in a variety of **parenting and developmental topics** including: brain development, prenatal care, nutrition, discipline, routines, infant care, and home safety.
- Provide information and **answer parent questions**, while also **introducing activities** that parents can do with their babies and toddlers to promote brain development and growth.
- Embrace the importance of working with **both parent and child**, with knowledge imparted on the parent so that it can be reinforced with the child.

In addition to Baby Coaching, Parent Universe offers customized in-home classes for expecting couples on topics such as: Childbirth Education, Breastfeeding Education, and Infant Care and Safety. Moreover, Parent Universe hosts a website with free resources that can be accessed by the public. Finally, Parent Universe hosts periodic community events ranging in scope and price from parenting workshops to author talks.

APPENDIX 3 171

Market Demand and Opportunity

Parent Universe targets parents with the means to afford Baby Coaching and related parent support services. Additionally, we will target large corporations to offer Baby Coaching as part of a competitive employee benefit package. A portion of proceeds would be used to make services available across all income brackets, thereby increasing the availability of supportive services to all NJ residents.

There is a growing trend in high-end services for parents. In upper-income communities, personal services such as baby nurses, baby planners, birthing doulas, and pregnancy concierges are gaining in popularity. There is a key opportunity to introduce Baby Coaching as a supportive service for parents that also encourages optimal growth and development of the child.

Likewise, Baby Coaching is an attractive service to corporations who are competing to attract and retain working mothers and fathers who now make up a substantial portion of the workforce and are struggling to balance work and family life. The workplace is changing. Today, more parents than ever before are juggling work and family life. According to the Bureau of Labor Statistics, in 2012 65% of mothers with children under age six were in the workforce. In 2011, among married-couple families with children under age six, 53% had both parents employed. Moms and dads alike are navigating a new world where trying to achieve work–family balance can be daunting. Large corporations in NJ are currently offering a number of benefits to attract family-oriented employees including: flexible hours, work-from-home options, child care assistance, car seat programs, and lactation facilities. Parent Universe's Baby Coaching services are a perfect addition to enhance the benefits package for these organizations and give them a competitive edge in acquiring the best possible workforce.

The ultimate goal of Parent Universe is to make home visiting and parent support services acceptable and available to all parents in New Jersey regardless of socioeconomic status. Our first step was to bring home-based services (Baby Coaching and related services) to the communities of suburban Essex and Morris Counties. We recently expanded to offer Baby Coaching in Middlesex, Mercer, Burlington, and Somerset Counties. We plan to expand to additional communities in New Jersey

172 APPENDIX 3

as well as pursue corporate contracts. We will also gradually expand upon our services to include additional parenting workshops and community events. Next we will expand to center-based services that promote positive parent–child interaction and parental support such as parent support groups, lactation support groups, and parent–child classes (yoga, music, etc.). Finally, we will use our influence to advocate for policies that support parents and foster the growth of our parenting services.

Social Impact

Investments made in children in the earliest years—as early as prenatally —have been found to have the strongest impact on lifelong health and well-being. The period from 0–3 represents the most significant time period in terms of rapid brain development and establishing a lifelong health trajectory.[2] Parents who invest in their children early on can expect to see a return in terms of higher educational achievement, stronger immune systems and disease resistance, better physical and emotional health, and less likelihood to be involved in negative behaviors (e.g. criminal activity and substance abuse).[2] The Washington State Institute for Public Policy reports that some established home visitation programs achieve a benefit-to-cost ratio of up to \$6.06 social return on every dollar invested.[8] These calculations take into consideration savings in terms of healthcare, child welfare, criminal justice, special education, and productivity losses.[5] It has been said that "children's health is a nation's wealth."[2] Investments in children today will lead to a more intelligent and competent workforce to compete in the global economy of the future. Consider the following benefits of strengthening early childhood experiences that have been found through research and program evaluation.

Health Benefits:
- Healthier birth weight
- Better developmental outcomes
- Better behavioral outcomes
- Stronger immune systems and greater disease resistance
- Better mental health
- Reduced substance abuse

Educational Benefits:
- Higher cognitive and vocabulary scores
- Higher test scores on math and reading
- Higher grade point averages
- Early detection of developmental delays reduces the need for special education services

Productivity Gains:
- Less stress for parents
- Better sleep patterns for children, which lead to better sleep for parents and more productive employees
- Healthier children mean less sick days for parent employees
- Children earn higher wages as adults
- Reduced criminal activity

DESCRIPTION OF THE ENTERPRISE

Parent Universe is the perfect marriage between a social service movement and a market trend. Home visitation is widely regarded as the gold standard in child abuse prevention, and leaders in the field support the expansion of home visiting services beyond the scope of "high-risk" clients to universal accessibility. At the same time, there is a growing trend in high-end services for parents. In upper-income communities, personal services such as baby nurses, baby planners, birthing doulas, and pregnancy concierges are gaining in popularity. For us, this is the perfect opportunity to introduce home visitation into the mainstream in the form of a profitable commodity.

Public policies in the US have been based on the assumption that private, informal networks are sufficient to help most parents care for their children. But being a new parent can be stressful and overwhelming even for those with a number of resources on hand. The government generally funds parenting support services only for low-income families, teen parents, families dealing with a disability, and families otherwise considered vulnerable or at-risk.

Parent Universe seeks to change this mindset. We believe that ALL parents, regardless of age, race, or socioeconomic status, need support and guidance at and around the time of birth to get them started in the right direction and help to ensure that their children get off to a good start and have healthy, happy, and safe childhoods.

The mission of Parent Universe is to support new parents during the exciting time surrounding the birth of a baby. Parent Universe provides a variety of home-based supportive services to families during pregnancy and throughout the first three years of a child's life.

The vision for Parent Universe is for all parents in New Jersey to have access to supportive services to help them during the transition to parenthood. To achieve this vision, proceeds from the sales of Baby Coaching and other services will be used to enhance the services of Prevent Child Abuse New Jersey, which provides services to low-income and vulnerable families. Additionally, funds will be used to address gaps in services and other underserved communities as they are identified.

APPENDIX 3

Our Services

Our signature service, Baby Coaching, consists of customized one-on-one sessions to assist parents with encouraging optimal growth and development of their child. Baby Coaches are certified Parent Educators who have completed a training program in the evidence-informed *Parents As Teachers (PAT)* curriculum (the same foundational training and curriculum used by state-funded home visitation programs). Baby Coaches:

- Meet with parents in the convenience of their own home.
- Provide educational sessions tailored to the family's wishes.
- Have expertise in a variety of parenting and developmental topics including: brain development, prenatal care, nutrition, discipline, routines, infant care, and home safety.
- Provide information and answer parent questions, while also introducing activities that parents can do with their babies and toddlers to promote brain development and growth. All activities incorporate the three areas of emphasis in the PAT curriculum: parent-child interaction, development-centered parenting, and family well-being.
- Embrace the importance of working with both parent and child, with knowledge imparted on the parent so that it can be reinforced with the child.

In addition to Baby Coaching, Parent Universe offers customized in-home classes for expecting couples on topics such as: Childbirth Education, Breastfeeding Education, and Infant Care and Safety. Moreover, Parent Universe hosts a website with free resources that can be accessed by the public. Finally, Parent Universe hosts periodic community events ranging in scope and price from parenting workshops to author talks.

Our Innovative Approach

Parent Universe is an innovative approach to preventing child maltreatment because services are framed as non-threatening, supportive, and available to all families regardless of perceived risk of child maltreatment. In today's society, there is a stigma associated with parents receiving supportive services. Parent Universe combats that stigma by marketing a high-end customized service that supports families in the comfort of their own homes. Through the appeal of improved health and development of the child, we reach parents during a stressful time in their lives. Parent Universe builds upon the parents' knowledge in a trusting and supportive relationship that ultimately enhances parental confidence and decreases the likelihood of child abuse or neglect.

Our team of professionals will adapt existing program models that have been proven effective with low-income and at-risk families to:

- improve school readiness
- improve child health and well-being
- improve parental health and well-being
- increase parenting confidence
- reduce the incidence of child abuse and neglect

These are outcomes that any parent would want for their child. We will be first to offer these services to a clientele with the means to purchase them.

Key Innovations

Parent Universe is unique in both focus and structure. First, our focus is three-tiered with emphasis on the parent, the child, and the parent-child relationship. Therefore, as outlined earlier, our services are designed to have positive outcomes across all three tiers. Furthermore, we are not limited to work with families during infancy. Our services are appropriate during pregnancy, during infancy, and throughout the complicated changes that occur in toddlerhood. We focus on the first three years of the child's life as this is a critical time for rapid growth and brain development. The early stages of parenting are also the ideal time to clarify expectations, build parental confidence, and address the fear that comes with lack of experience. The time from birth to age three also represents the riskiest time for children in terms of child maltreatment, as parents are often overwhelmed and frustrated with the dependency of very young children.

Second, we are unique in structure when compared to others in the field. An analysis of the market shows that most area professionals providing postpartum services are operating individually or in pairs. These teams of only one or two women fulfill all of the administrative functions of the company as well as providing the home-based services. While overhead is low, this structure prevents the ability to reach a high volume of clients, and perhaps compromises the quality of the administrative functions. In fact, in our research we interviewed two of these independent home-based providers separately, and both reported that the time devoted to marketing and administration was a primary challenge. One of these providers even reported that corporations and pediatricians would have contracted with her for a high volume of services if she had a team of employees rather than a single-person operation. To set us apart, our structure consists of a dedicated director to fulfill the administrative functions, including quality assurance and oversight of the Baby Coaches. This allows our Baby Coaches to concentrate fully on providing the highest quality services to our clients. It also allows us to grow as our client pool increases so that we may expand to additional communities. Furthermore, with a structure that adapts easily to growth and volume, we also gain the ability to offer a range of services at varying costs so that our services can ultimately be universally accessible.

Finally, Parent Universe services appeal to parents who need support for a specific need or a temporary trying time in their lives, such as help during transition back to work, getting a baby to sleep, learning to cope with toddler tantrums, or preparing a young child for the birth of a sibling. Traditional home visitation services that require a long-term commitment of weekly or monthly visits may be too intensive for these parents.

Theory of Change

Our hypothesis is that promoting services such as those offered by Parent Universe will contribute to a shift in the way the public views parent support services such as home visitation. Research conducted by sociologist Rebecca Kissane (2003) found that stigma plays a key role in the refusal to utilize available social services among low-income mothers. Psychologist Ron Prinz (2009) agrees that parenting services that are targeted (e.g. home visitation for at-risk families) as opposed to universal (e.g. childbirth education classes) carry the stigma of being intended for parents who are failing or expected to fail at parenting. Note that in countries where universal home visitation is the norm, outcomes for maternal and child health are far better than in the US, including much lower rates of child maltreatment (Cawthorne & Arons, 2010; ECMF, 2010). Introducing Baby Coaching and related services into the marketplace will help to normalize parent support services, making them more desirable and acceptable to parents and the general public.

Mission Statement

The mission of Parent Universe is to support new parents during the exciting time surrounding the birth of a baby. Parent Universe provides a variety of home-based supportive services to families during pregnancy and throughout the first three years of a child's life. Our signature service, Baby Coaching, includes customized one-on-one sessions to assist parents with encouraging optimal growth and development of their child. All services are offered à la carte, so families on nearly any budget can access the help they need. Our goal is to ensure that children and parents get off to the best possible start.

The vision for Parent Universe is for all parents in New Jersey to have access to supportive services to help them during the transition to parenthood. To achieve this vision, proceeds from the sales of Baby Coaching and other services will be put toward sliding scale and subsidized services for low-income families, the development of free online resources for all parents, and advocacy for programs and policies that support all families in NJ.

Core Values

We believe that parents are the most important influence in their children's growth and development. Parents have the unique capacity to nurture, nourish, and mold children with intellectual curiosity, moral character, and healthy self-esteem.

We believe that children learn in the context of relationships, and thrive with consistent positive and stimulating parent-child inter-action.

We believe that all parents need support and guidance to meet the complex needs of their children and families. In today's society, extended families are often separated by distance and life circumstances. We aim to supplement the role of the extended family in supporting new and expectant parents.

Goals and Measurement

Parent Universe has a double-bottom line. First, we aim to be fully self-sustainable through earned income. Our earned income will come through the following mechanisms:

- Baby Coaching sessions (standard 60-minute sessions).
- Customized home visiting sessions (variable price).
- Lactation consultation sessions.
- Nutrition consultation sessions.
- Attendance to parent workshops.
- Partnerships with corporations (explained later in Competitive Advantage).
- Contracts with corporations (explained later in Competitive Advantage).

The long-term social impact of Parent Universe is to prevent child abuse and neglect through the provision of services that support and educate parents.

To achieve this impact, we have set the following social goals and objectives:

- Goal #1: Increase the accessibility and availability of parent support services in NJ.
  - Objective: Use Baby Coaching to reach new populations that currently do not have access to supportive services.
  - Objective: Use marketing to increase the awareness among the community about parent support services.
  - Objective: Use marketing to improve the public image as it relates to parent support services.

- Goal #2: Educate and support parents with children ages 0–3.
  - Objective: Increase parental confidence.
  - Objective: Increase knowledge of parenting and child development.

To measure our progress toward achieving our first goal and corresponding objectives, we will conduct a survey among NJ pediatricians and birthing professionals. We have already conducted a survey through the NJ Chapter of the American Academy of Pediatrics, which yielded valuable data from 29 pediatricians and two pediatric nurse practitioners. We are also connected through PCANJ programming to a network of birthing professionals in Essex County and the surrounding areas, which enabled us to reach 27 professionals in a survey we conducted in 2012. We are confident that we will be able to gather valuable data through these same networks to assess the impact of Parent Universe. We intend to conduct a pre-test survey in our first fiscal year and a post-test survey in our second fiscal year. A draft of this survey is attached in Appendix C. Furthermore, we will collect data to determine if there is an increase in the number of parents reached, the number of communities/municipalities served, and the number and type of referral sources.

To measure our progress toward achieving our second goal, we will conduct a brief eight-item pre-test survey with all parents prior to the first Baby Coaching session. The survey will be given to the parents again following the completion of three Baby Coaching sessions (when applicable). Questions from the survey have been adapted from standardized, validated, and reliable instruments. In an effort to increase the response rate and avoid uneasiness among our customers, we have selected key non-threatening questions to compile this short survey. The survey is included in Appendix D.

Social Return on Investment

Investments in children in the earliest years—as early as prenatally—have been found to have the strongest impact on lifelong health and well-being. The period from 0–3 represents the most significant time period in terms of rapid brain development and establishing a lifelong health trajectory.[2] Parents who invest in our services can expect to see a return in their children in terms of higher educational achievement, stronger immune systems and disease resistance, better physical and emotional health, and less likelihood to be involved in negative behaviors (e.g. criminal activity and substance abuse).[2] On a societal level, it has been said that "children's health is a nation's wealth"[2] as investments in children today will lead to a more intelligent and competent workforce to compete in the global economy of the future. The Washington State Institute for Public Policy reports that some established home visitation programs achieve a benefit-to-cost ratio ranging from $1.18 to $6.06 social return on every dollar invested.[8] These calculations take into consideration benefits that primarily stem from the prevention of child maltreatment. Child maltreatment has been found to lead to lifelong adverse effects in terms of physical health, mental health, criminal activity, educational performance, and economic security.[5] It has been conservatively estimated that the societal costs over the lifetime of a child abuse survivor is $210,000, while the lifetime cost to society for a child abuse death is $1,272,900.[5] These figures take into consideration the costs of healthcare, child welfare, criminal justice, special education, and productivity losses.[5] At the core of home visitation programs is the goal to prevent child abuse and neglect. The home visitation models that serve as the template for Parent Universe have all been rigorously tested and found to reduce the incidence of child abuse and neglect among program participants.

The effect of expanding home visitation to a larger demographic is expected to increase the acceptance of home visitation among at-risk clients. Leaders in the field agree that universal accessibility of home visitation eliminates stigma and increases the appeal of such services to at-risk parents.[3]

Competitive Advantage

One of our goals is to be financially self-sustaining through earned income after the first year. Therefore, our initial focus is to acquire sufficient start-up funds to employ part-time administrative office staff and to train per diem Baby Coaches. For start-up funds, we will be looking primarily for advances on contracts from large corporations, and also for investments from social venture capitalists or philanthropists. We also have the option of applying for a bank loan.

Parent Universe is designed to be fully self-sufficient with full-time administrative staff through earned income once we reach a critical mass of 4,000 Baby Coaching sessions per year. To reach this capacity, we will look for opportunities to reach clients in large volume using the following strategies:

- Negotiate contracts with large corporations to include home visiting services as part of a competitive benefits package. We will target the nine corporations in New Jersey that were named as the Best Companies for Working Mothers in 2012: Automatic Data Processing, Horizon Healthcare Services, Inc., Johnson and Johnson, Merck, Novartis Pharmaceuticals, Pearson, Prudential Financial, Rothstein Kass, and Unilever.
- We are exploring the possibility of getting reimbursed through health insurance companies or flexible spending accounts in the same way that other wellness programs are often reimbursed (e.g. gym memberships, weight loss programs, smoking cessation programs). There are data showing that home visitation programs have a number of positive impacts on the health of the mother and baby in terms of immunizations, well-baby visits, prenatal care, postpartum care, perinatal depression, reduced emergency room care, and reduced child abuse and neglect.
- We will offer membership plans and packages of services that can be purchased by the parent, or by a loved one looking for a gift for the parent. Packages will promote the sale of multiple visits/services at one time.

Additionally, we will look for other opportunities to bring in revenue outside the scope of our home-based services using the following strategies:

- Partner with corporations who may have a desire to market to our clients. This can be in the form of advertisements on our websites, donated product samples, sponsorship of program materials, or fees for information sharing.

- Offer services that corporations can purchase to provide to staff in-house as part of a competitive benefits package. These services include: on-site workshops on topics related to parenting challenges, and on-site parent support groups or lactation support groups.
- To supplement our home-based services, we will hold special events throughout the year. These events will be marketed to our home visiting clients and will include parent workshops, author talks, and educational sessions for birthing and early childhood professionals.

Inaction

One of our goals is to cause a shift in public perception of parenting services and to increase demand for home-based support around the time of childbirth. Since home visitation services are scarce, varied, and small-scale, there is no precedent for a high demand of these services. For this reason, we plan to focus substantial energy on marketing and relationship-building in order to increase the volume of our clients. Our marketing efforts will target both new/expectant parents and professionals who work in the birthing and parenting industries. Likewise, our Baby Coaches must be adept at sales and marketing. We understand that word of mouth can be a powerful marketing tool among our client population, so customer satisfaction is extremely important to us.

APPENDIX 3

THE TEAM AND ORGANIZATIONAL BACKGROUND

The Team

In order to be successful, we will need a strong administrative staff and well-trained and experienced Baby Coaches. The following is a description of the staffing structure we aim to build.

- **Director:** Full-time position that oversees the operations of the social venture. This person is responsible for hiring staff, managing staff, supervising the home visitors, marketing the services, networking, and negotiating contracts. This person is also responsible for organizing community events and parent workshops. All staff report to the director.
- **Assistant:** Full-time position responsible for answering phones, scheduling visits, assigning customers, and data entry and tracking. This person is also responsible for assisting with planning community events and parent workshops.
- **Baby Coach:** Per diem position to provide in-home services to customers. This person should have a minimum of a Bachelor's degree in social work, nursing, public health, psychology, or a related field. This person should have a minimum of five years of experience working with new or expectant parents. Applicants with certification as doula, lactation consultant, or childbirth educator preferred.
- **Website Manager:** Part-time position to create and maintain a sophisticated website with information about services, upcoming events, free resources, and blog. Also manages the Facebook page.
- **Accountant:** Part-time position to manage finances, process payments, and handle billing.

Patty Mojta is currently in the role of director. Patty is a licensed social worker who has been working with children and families for 10 years, mostly in the fields of early childhood development and parent education. Patty believes that in order for children to have the best chances in life, their parents need to be supported and nurtured. Patty has spent most of her career developing and implementing programs that support parents and families. As a proud mother of two boys, Patty knows the challenges of parenting firsthand and is appreciative for all of the support she had during her transition to parenthood. Now she is committed to helping other parents as they transition to the most challenging and rewarding phase of their lives.

Miriam Ruchman is currently in the role of Baby Coach and also provides administrative support. Miriam has a Master's degree in psychology, is a board certified lactation consultant, a Parents As Teachers educator, and a labor doula. Miriam has been assisting parents on their journey from pregnancy to infanthood and beyond since 2002. Her most challenging yet gratifying role is mothering her two teenage daughters. She believes that parents deserve compassionate support and evidence-based strategies and information to strengthen the health and happiness of their families.

About Prevent Child Abuse New Jersey

Parent Universe is an earned-income social venture of the nonprofit organization Prevent Child Abuse New Jersey (PCANJ). PCANJ is the statewide headquarters for two national evidence-based home visitation program models, and oversees these and a variety of other primary and secondary prevention programs.

As employees of Prevent Child Abuse New Jersey, the developers of this enterprise have significant expertise in evidence-based home visitation programs, program design and evaluation, and partnership building. We also design and conduct trainings for professionals and parents on topics related to parenting, child development, and working with families. As the state affiliate for two nationally acclaimed evidence-based home visitation models (Healthy Families America and Parents As Teachers), our agency employs certified trainers in home visitation and parenting education. We are the only agency in the state to host the Parents As Teachers training for parent educator certification, which is a certification that all of our Baby Coaches maintain.

In addition, we operate a program at PCANJ that is charged with building relationships with birthing professionals in Essex County.

Through this program, we link new and expectant parents with state-funded home visitation and other supportive services. In our service delivery, we have built relationships with providers whose clientele are not eligible for state-funded home visitation due to geography and income level. Parent Universe provides services that fill this gap and meet the demands of NJ parents who do not currently have access to home visitation services.

Legal Structure

Parent Universe services are consistent with the agency's mission to prevent child abuse and neglect for all of New Jersey's children through the provision of parent support and educational programming. Parent Universe will operate under the umbrella of Prevent Child Abuse New Jersey. Prevent Child Abuse New Jersey will receive legal guidance from the Pro Bono Partnership. We may decide to incorporate as a for-profit corporation owned by Prevent Child Abuse New Jersey at some point in the future.

Current Status

We are currently in the launch phase. We are fully prepared to offer Baby Coaching and Lactation Consultation sessions in Essex and Morris Counties, and have begun to implement our marketing strategies. Our goal in this first year of operation is to sell 100 Baby Coaching sessions.

Advisors

In addition to the expertise of PCANJ staff, we are in the process of forming an advisory board for Parent Universe. We have been receiving guidance and mentorship informally from a number of key stakeholders. As we move into the launch phase of this initiative, we are looking to formalize an advisory board with key members who can help grow the enterprise and promote our vision of a New Jersey where all parents have access to supportive services.

THE MARKET AND INDUSTRY

Industry Description and Market Segments

The State of New Jersey funds three models of evidence-based home visitation services: Healthy Families America, Nurse-Family Partnership, and Parents As Teachers. These programs have the capacity to serve approximately 3,000 families statewide–which is only 2.5% of the total annual births in NJ (New Jersey DCF Funded EBHV Programs and Capacity, 2010). Furthermore, in 2011, there were 9,414 substantiated cases of child abuse or neglect in New Jersey and an additional 91,680 investigations (State of New Jersey Department of Children and Families, 2011). These investigations represent additional families at risk for future child maltreatment. There is a clear need for additional home visitation services in New Jersey.

Moreover, the available home visitation services are overwhelmingly concentrated in low-income communities, criteria for enrollment is narrow, and families who enroll must commit to long-term intensive services. Therefore, these services rarely reach parents in middle- or upper-income brackets, and may be inaccessible or unappealing to eligible low-income families due to narrow enrollment criteria and the intensity of service delivery.

Fee-based services that exist are more accessible to middle- and upper-income parents. However, the majority of these services are center-based (e.g. childbirth education courses, parent support groups), target parents during the prenatal period only (e.g. birth doulas, Lamaze), and are not inclusive of all family members (e.g. Mommy and Me classes, breast-feeding support). Furthermore, none of these high-end services are grounded in child abuse prevention models.

In much of the industrialized world, universal home visitation is the norm. Countries such as Denmark, Finland, Germany, Great Britain, Ireland, Italy, the Netherlands, Norway, and Australia have widespread voluntary and free home visitation services built into their national healthcare system. These countries also have the lowest rates of child maltreatment and much better overall outcomes for maternal and child health. In contrast, the US ties with Mexico for the highest child abuse deaths among all industrialized nations—11 times that of Italy (Cawthorne & Arons, 2010; ECMF, 2010).

Parent Universe's Baby Coaching would be the first step in creating non-stigmatizing parent support services in New Jersey that are grounded in a child abuse prevention framework. The goal is to expand to include parenting classes, support groups, educational campaigns, and marketing strategies to further de-stigmatize and create demand for supportive services for new and expecting parents.

Target Market Segments

Our target market in the first year included middle- and upper-income parents in suburban Essex and Morris Counties. In Essex County, there are approximately 11,213 births annually. Of these births, 1,304 are born to residents in nine municipalities where more than 20% of the population have a household income of $200,000 or more (according to the 2010 U.S. Census). In Morris County, there are approximately 5,361 births annually. Of these births, 1,682 are born to residents in 14 municipalities where more than 20% of the population have a household income of $200,000 or more (according to the 2010 U.S. Census).

In Essex County, there are approximately 11,213 births annually. Of these births:

- 3,730 are born to first-time parents
- 3,446 are born to mothers with a college degree or higher
- 6,767 are born to mothers who are not on Medicaid
- 1,304 are born to residents in the municipalities of: Essex Fells, Glen Ridge, Livingston, Maplewood, Millburn, Montclair, South Orange, Short Hills, and Upper Montclair*

In Morris County, there are approximately 5,361 births annually. Of these births:

- 1,937 are born to first-time parents
- 3,131 are born to mothers with a college degree or higher
- 4,777 are to mothers who are not on Medicaid

---

*These municipalities all have more than 20% of the population with a household income of $200,000 or more (according to the U.S. Census).

- 1,682 are born to residents in the municipalities of: Boonton Town, Chatham Borough, Chatham Township, Chester Township, Harding, Kinnelon, Madison, Mendham Borough, Mendham Township, Montville, Morris Township, Mountain Lakes, Randolph, and Washington Township*

In order to become financially profitable, we need to reach a high volume of paying clients. Our secondary target market will be corporations and health insurance companies. We will try to be included in employee benefits packages, which will open up our services to a broader clientele of middle-income parents. Negotiating these contracts will be our primary course of action.

As we build a client base and grow to new communities, we aim to lower our costs so that our services can be accessible to a greater number of New Jersey residents. Our long-term goal is to be able to serve parents across all income brackets throughout the entire state of New Jersey.

Expected Position in Target Market Segments

In the spring of 2012, Parent Universe conducted research with professionals who work with expectant or newly parenting families, including pediatricians, nurses, doulas, childbirth educators, lactation consultants, and others to determine:

- The areas in which they feel clients/patients most need additional support.
- Their likelihood of referring families for that support.
- The likelihood of their clients/patients purchasing services on a fee-for-service basis.

Our research included 87 professionals serving clients across all 21 counties in New Jersey. Of these, 47% reported serving clients in Essex County and 17% reported serving clients in Morris County. More than half (54%) of the respondents reported serving middle-income families and more than one-quarter (28%) reported serving upper-income families.

The following—which are key areas Parent Universe will specialize in—were ranked highest as those in which families would need additional support:

- Knowledge of infant care (73%)
- Breastfeeding (73%)
- Basic parenting skills (71%)
- Stress management and coping (65%)
- Knowledge of child development (63%)
- Nutrition for baby (63%)
- Positive discipline strategies (63%)

Also ranked high (by 50% or more of all respondents) were the areas of soothing a crying baby, preparing for a baby's birth, nutrition for mother, sleeping/naptime routines, and linkages to local resources.

An overwhelming 80% said they would be "very likely" or "somewhat likely" to refer families for additional support in these areas and one-third felt their clients/patients were "very likely" or "somewhat likely" to purchase services.

How likely are you to make a referral for your clients/patients to receive additional support in the above areas? (n = 86)

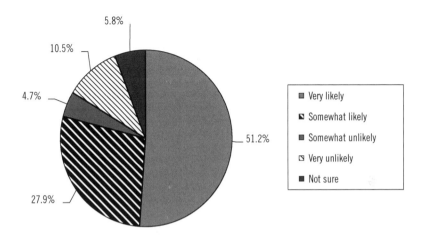

How likely do you feel it would be for your clients/patients to purchase fee-based services to address these areas? (n = 87)

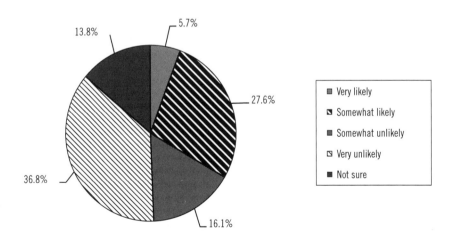

192   APPENDIX 3

MARKETING PLAN

Fundraising Targets and Strategies

For our purposes, fundraising and marketing are one and the same. We will have a comprehensive marketing strategy that includes traditional advertising, networking, and negotiating contracts.

Products and Pricing Plan

Suggested price points:

- Baby Coaching: $125 per one-hour visit; offer packages with bulk discounts (i.e. five visits for $525)
- Prenatal classes: variable, $199–549 (one to three sessions)
- Parent workshops: variable, $10–100 per person
- Professional forums: variable, $50–100 per person

We also offer membership plans and package deals:

- Introductory Package: $325—includes three one-hour Baby Coaching sessions ($50 savings)
- Deluxe Package: $525—includes five one-hour Baby Coaching sessions ($100 savings)
- Premium Package: $1,000—includes 10 one-hour Baby Coaching sessions ($250 savings)
- Build Your Own Package: prices vary
- 6-Month Membership Plan: $99 per month for one Baby Coaching session per month plus 10% discount on all additional purchases
- 12-Month Membership Plan: $99 per month for one Baby Coaching session per month plus 10% discount on all additional purchases

Placement and Promotion

Our target market includes middle- and upper-income families in Essex and Morris Counties, as well as large companies looking to attract and retain working parents.

We will target several populations:

1. Individual customers
2. Friends/relatives of potential customers
3. Professionals who work with potential customers
4. Corporations

In order to reach potential clients, we advertise in popular local magazines and on popular parenting websites, including NJ Baby magazine and NJFamily.com. We joined professional organizations such as milkzip.org so that we can be easily located through Web searches. We advertise our workshops and speaking engagements in local online newspapers. We maintain a professional and comprehensive website and Facebook page, and we have produced high-quality brochures that can be distributed by our partners.

Additionally, we offer packages and membership plans that can be purchased as a gift for the new or expectant parent. We will market these options to grandparents who may not be physically able to support their children and grandchildren. To reach this audience, we will advertise in newspapers and magazines that target seniors.

It is important to increase awareness of our services among birthing and parenting professionals by providing information sessions and setting up exhibit tables at professional conferences. We will build upon current relationships with birthing professionals in the community, as well as foster new relationships with maternal and child educators in the area hospitals and local pediatricians.

Finally, as described earlier, we feel that the volume of clients can best be reached through negotiating contracts with corporations and health insurance companies. This will expand our target population to a broader income base. To achieve success in this area, we will use personal connections to set up meetings with corporate decision-makers and private insurance providers. We will offer lunch-and-learn sessions to corporations to educate employees about parenting-related topics and our services. Upon the conclusion of these sessions, we will survey the employees about the interest in our services, and use this data to encourage employers to contract with us. We will also offer the option of cost sharing with employers in which a majority (e.g. 80%) of the costs of Baby Coaching sessions is paid by the employer with a small co-pay paid by the employee.

A detailed marketing plan is attached in Appendix G.

A corporate proposal is included in Appendix H of this document.

We are confident that our services will appeal to our market and afford us the opportunity to achieve our goals. There is a growing body of research supporting home-based parent support services as an effective way to move outcomes that are important to parents, employers, and other stakeholders. Consider the following outcomes supported by research:

Examples of outcomes that appeal to parents:

- A study of the Healthy Families home visitation program found that mothers who received home visits during pregnancy were half as likely to deliver low birth weight babies compared to mothers in the control group (Healthy Families New York; The PEW Center on the States, 2010). Low birth weight is associated with greater risk for obesity, diabetes, and cardio-vascular disease (Center on the Developing Child at Harvard University, 2010).
- Another study of the Healthy Families home visitation program found that children who had received home visits had better developmental and behavioral outcomes compared with children in the control group (Gonzalez & MacMillan, 2008).

Examples of outcomes that appeal to employers:

- A study of Early Head Start programs found that mothers who participated in home visits reported less stress than mothers in the control group (The PEW Center on the States, 2010).
- Positive parenting during early infancy promotes the strengthening of the child's immune system (Center on the Developing Child at Harvard University, 2010). Less sick days for baby mean less sick days for mom and dad!

THE FINANCIAL PLAN

Fiscal oversight for Parent Universe will be provided by the manager of financial operations, the accounting clerk, the finance committee of the board of directors, and an annual agency audit.

Start-up funds provided by the PCANJ Opportunity Fund and JR Consulting Services were used for: training of one Baby Coach, printing brochures and advertising materials, purchasing home visiting materials, and supporting a phone line and website for Parent Universe. Additional start-up funds were awarded by the New Jersey Office of Faith-Based Initiatives to support: hiring and training additional Baby Coaches, advertising in the media, purchasing promotional materials, purchasing home visiting materials and educational equipment, and setting up lunch and learns with providers who will be referral sources for customers.

Our Year 1 Income Statement (Appendix H) projects positive gains of $7,403. A five-year projected income statement, attached in Appendix I, shows that we project consistent growth and positive gains without further infusion of grant funds after the start-up year. In Year 1, we will focus on marketing Baby Coaching sessions in Essex and Morris Counties with a goal of selling 100 sessions. We will also focus on building a professional website that generates income through advertising. By Year 2, we will begin marketing in-home prenatal classes as well as expand our reach with Baby Coaching sessions. By Year 3, we project a 50% growth rate of in-home services, as well as the introduction of workshops, community events, and corporate partnerships. In order to stay on target with our growth projections, we will gradually increase the amount of dedicated staff time on this project. The goal is to build to a full-time director of Parent Universe and full-time assistant over a period of five to seven years. We will be able to fund these positions fully once we reach a capacity of 4,000 in-home sessions annually, or any combination of other income sources that yields the same amount of income.

OPERATIONS PLAN

Definition of Success

The vision for Parent Universe is for all parents in New Jersey to have access to supportive services to help them during the transition to parenthood.

Intermediate Goals and Success Measures

Our first goal is to bring home-based services (Baby Coaching and related services) to the communities of suburban Essex and Morris Counties.

We will then expand to additional communities in New Jersey. We will also gradually expand upon our services to include parenting workshops and community events.

Next, we will expand to center-based services that promote positive parent-child interaction and parental support such as parent support groups, lactation support groups, and parent-child classes (yoga, music, etc.).

We will also use our influence to advocate for policies that support parents and foster the growth of our parenting services.

Timeline

Thus far in our first year, Parent Universe has employed a Baby Coach who is a certified lactation consultant. This staff member has successfully completed initial training within one to three months of being hired. Also during this time period, policies, marketing materials, and a website were developed, and marketing strategies and service delivery were established. By the twelfth month, Parent Universe will expand services to additional counties in NJ. At this time, Parent Universe will begin targeting corporations with marketing strategies and begin selling ad space on the website.

In the second year, Parent Universe will begin to focus on growth and expansion. By 60 months of operation, the venture aims to acquire office space for center-based services and advocate for policies that support parents and parenting services. This timeline demonstrates the action steps required for Parent Universe to become self-sustainable.

APPENDIX 3

A detailed outline of the timeline is stated below.

Month 0	Start date (incorporation)
Month 0–2	Hire staff
	Acquire space
	Acquire equipment
Month 1–3	Initial training of staff
	Develop policies
	Develop marketing materials
	Build website
Month 3	Initiate marketing strategies and begin service delivery
	Beginning of cash flow
Month 12	Expand services to include in-home prenatal classes
	Begin targeting corporations with marketing strategies
	Begin selling ad space on website
Month 24	Expand to five new home visitors
	Start serving new communities
	Begin holding community events and workshops
Month 36	Expand to eight home visitors
	Start serving new communities
Month 60	Expand to 12 home visitors
	Start serving new communities
	Acquire office space for center-based services
	Advocate for policies that support parents and parenting services

RISK ASSESSMENT

Financial Risk

The greatest financial risk for our endeavor is the need for a high volume of clients in order for the venture to be financially self-sustaining. Our overhead costs are much higher than other home-based parenting services, which means that we need to have a high volume of clients being served by a team of coaches. Fortunately, our infrastructure enables us to grow to this capacity. This is in contrast to other independent home-based service providers, whose small size leads to limited and missed opportunities.

Additionally, we plan to increase our client base through creative strategies that target group sales rather than individual sales. These strategies include:

- We plan to target corporations to be added as a competitive employee benefit.
- We are also exploring the possibility of becoming a reimbursable expense through health insurance or flexible spending accounts.
- Finally, we will also sell services in the form of "packages" and membership plans that can be purchased as a gift.

Legal Risk

As part of a nonprofit organization, it is important that our earned-income activities remain directly in line with the organization's social mission. There are also limitations to how much revenue we can generate with our activities. We obtain legal guidance through the Pro Bono Partnership to ensure that our decisions and activities are within the legal limits. At some point in the future, we may decide to incorporate as a separate entity.

Talent Risk

We run the risk of losing our Baby Coaching staff who may be enticed to pursue a career independent from our company. They may see the opportunity to be paid $125 per visit as more appealing than working for our per diem rate. However, we have built a structure that protects us somewhat from this risk by paying our Baby Coaches a competitive wage. Additionally, we invest only minimally (less than $1,000) in the hiring and training of a new Baby Coach.

Environmental Risk

As with all businesses that operate within the marketplace, Parent Universe will be vulnerable to economic downturns that limit the consumer's disposable income. To mitigate this risk, we plan to contract with corporations as a primary strategy to build a secure customer base.

SUPPORTING DOCUMENTS

Appendix A: Child Abuse in the U.S.*

Appendix B: Organizational Chart of Parent Universe

Appendix C: Logic Model*

Appendix D: Survey of Birth Professionals

Appendix E: Customer Survey

Appendix F: Resume of Social Entrepreneur

Appendix G: Marketing Plan

Appendix H: Corporate Proposal

Appendix I: Year 1 Income Statement

Appendix J: 5-Year Income Statement*

References

---

*These appendices are included in this book. All other appendices are available from the book's author upon request.

APPENDIX A: CHILD ABUSE IN THE U.S.

Few realize the grim outlook for children born in the United States when compared to the remainder of the developed world. The US ties with Mexico for the highest child abuse deaths among all industrialized nations—triple that of Canada and 11 times that of Italy.[1,4] While we lament the loss of U.S. forces killed in the past decade of wars in Iraq and Afghanistan, it is almost impossible to imagine that we have lost almost four times as many children in the same time frame due to abuse and neglect.[4]

In terms of child well-being, what separates the United States from the rest of the industrialized world is a lack of parent support services. Universal healthcare and universal home visitation is the norm in much of the industrialized world, including all of Western and Northern Europe.[1,9] These countries that provide home visiting to all newborn children also have the lowest rates of child maltreatment and much better overall outcomes for maternal and child health.[1]

Home visiting services are so popular in Europe that, in general, their formal evaluation has not been deemed necessary. Legislators and scholars in Europe point to the positive health outcomes, relative to global comparisons, as evidence of the value of home visitation. Despite financial difficulty in most of these countries, funding for universal home visitation has never been in jeopardy, and its value has not been fodder for political debates. In fact, the concept of a targeted approach (limited to low-income or at-risk families) rather than universal accessibility goes against the convictions of Europeans who believe that labeling home visitation in this way would stigmatize the service and turn people away from accepting the help.[8]

On the contrary, home visiting services are available on a much more limited scale in the United States, and virtually all home visiting programs are targeted to populations that are deemed "at-risk." In New Jersey, state-funded home visiting programs are overwhelmingly concentrated in low-income communities. Furthermore, legislators in the US rely heavily on scientific evaluation of home visiting services to ensure that taxpayer dollars are invested in worthwhile programs. As a result, home visitation and similar parent support services carry with them the stigma of being targeted to wayward or failed parents. However, poverty is not the only risk factor for abuse, and child maltreatment spans all income brackets. The stress associated with caring for a newborn affects all parents. For this reason, we argue that home visiting services should be universally available to all families at the time of childbirth.

In 1978, physician and noted child abuse expert C. Henry Kemp advocated for a universal home health visitation system reaching women during pregnancy and extending into the preschool years. In 1991, the U.S. Advisory Board on Child Abuse and Neglect recommended a universal home visiting program to prevent child abuse and neglect. Ten years later, universal home visiting in the U.S., let alone in a progressive state such as New Jersey, remains to be seen. There is a lack of understanding about home visiting and prevention programs in general, which are viewed by some as invasive or as the government "telling parents what to do."

To put this in perspective, consider attitudes about court-appointed parenting classes offered through a local charity. These services are often viewed as programs designed for ignorant or negligent parents—for parents who have failed at parenting. Now, consider attitudes about childbirth education classes. The perception is that parents who attend these classes are loving, attentive, and trying to learn about how to take good care of their new baby. Both programs aim to educate and support parents, with the result being improved parenting skills. The difference in perception stems from the monetary value associated with one program. It is our belief that parents who view themselves as good parents would also pay for home visiting services.

Baby Coaching would be the first step in creating non-stigmatizing parent support services. The goal is to expand to include parenting classes, support groups, educational campaigns, and marketing strategies to further de-stigmatize and create demand for supportive services for new and expecting parents.

APPENDIX C: LOGIC MODEL

Appendix C: Logic Model

Inputs	Goals	Objectives	Activities/Services	Outputs (Measured)	Outcomes (Measured)	Impacts
• Staff • Equipment • Relationships • Training • Space • Insurance • Materials • Database	1. Increase the accessibility and availability of parent support services in NJ	1. Use Baby Coaching to reach new populations that currently do not have access to supportive services 2. Use marketing to increase the awareness among the community about parent support services 3. Use marketing to improve the public image as it relates to parent support services	• FFS Home-Based Services • Subsidized or Sliding Scale Home-Based Services • Professional Forums • Marketing/Advertising • Partnerships with birthing professionals and pediatricians	• Geographic description of service population • Number/percentage of subsidized services/visits • Number/attendance of professional forums • Number of referrals • Number of referral sources • Number of official partnerships	• Increase in awareness of available services (survey) • Increase in referrals from new sources/communities • Policy changes within corporations that support working parents	De-stigmatize Parent Support Services

	2. Educate and support parents with children ages 0–3	1. Increase parental confidence
		2. Increase knowledge of parenting and child development
			• Home-Based Services (0–3):
			  o Baby Coaching
			  o In-home prenatal classes
			• Additional Services
			  o Online resources
			  o Parent workshops
			  o Author talks
				• Number of home visits
				• Breakdown of services provided
				• Number of parent workshops
				• Number of community events
				• Website/Facebook hits/traffic/"likes"
				• Demographics of service population
				• Client satisfaction
					• Increased Parental Confidence (questions 1, 2, 3, 6, and 7 from survey)
					• Increase in Parenting Knowledge/Knowledge of Child Development (questions 4 and 8 from survey)
						Prevent Child Abuse and Neglect

	3. Be financially sustainable through earned income strategies	1. Financially self-sustainable by 12 months 2. 20% profit margin by second year 3. Re-invest 50% of profits into growth of social venture	• FFS Home Based Services • Parent Workshops • Community events (i.e. author talks) • Sell advertising space on website • Partner with corporations to share information • Contract with corporations as employee benefit	• Amount raised • Income breakdown by service/activity	• Financially selfsustainable by 12 months • 20% profit margin by second year • Re-invest 50% of profits into growth of social venture	Make parent support services universally available to all NJ families

APPENDIX J: 5-YEAR INCOME STATEMENT

Parent Universe | 5-Year Pro Forma Income Statement

	Year 1	Year 2	Year 3	Year 4	Year 5
Income ($)					
Opportunity Fund - Seed Investment	5,625	0	0	0	0
JR Consulting Seed Investment	500				
OFBI SE2D Grant	23,000	0	0	0	0
Retained Income from Prior Year		3,701	614	284	1,314
Baby Coaching sessions ($125 per hour)	12,500	18,750	28,125	42,188	63,281
Prenatal Classes (1-session $199)	0	1,990	2,985	4,478	6,716
Prenatal Classes (3-session $549)	0	4,392	6,588	9,882	14,823
Workshop Attendance ($25 per ticket)	0	0	2,500	3,750	5,625
Advertising on Website	250	275	303	333	366
Corporate Partnerships	0	2,000	2,400	2,880	3,456
Total Income	41,875	31,108	43,514	63,794	95,581
Expense ($)					
Personnel					
Agency Staff	5,118	7,677	11,516	17,273	25,910
Baby Coach-BC session (no fringe)	5,500	8,250	12,375	18,563	27,844
Baby Coach-1-session class (no fringe)	0	920	1,380	2,070	3,105
Baby Coach-3-session class (no fringe)	0	2,208	3,312	4,968	7,452
Fringe (28.63%)	1,465	2,198	3,297	4,945	7,418
Subtotal Personnel	12,083	21,253	31,879	47,819	71,729
Other than Personnel					
Equipment	400	500	500	500	500
Professional Development/Training	3,000	1,780	1,780	1,780	1,780
Consultant	5,908	0	0	0	0
HV Materials	1,400	500	500	500	500
Database Upgrades	2,000	1,000	1,000	1,000	1,000
Website Hosting	25	25	25	25	25
Travel	2,000	500	500	500	500
Printing	1,225	500	500	500	500
Trademarking	100	0	0	0	0
Employment Advertising	250	50	50	50	50
Food and Materials	1,000	200	200	200	200
Advertising	1,947	857	857	857	857
Workshops	0	0	1,250	1,875	2,813
Subtotal Other than Personnel	19,255	5,912	7,162	7,787	8,725
Overhead Expenses (10%)	3,134	2,716	3,904	5,561	8,045
Total Expense	34,472	29,881	42,946	61,167	88,498
Net Income ($)	7,403	1,227	568	2,627	7,083
Retained Income - Parent Universe	3,701	614	284	1,314	3,541
PCANJ	3,701	614	284	1,314	3,541

Note: Parent Universe is projected to be self-sustaining after the first year of operation without the further infusion of grant funds. Positive gains are predicted that will grow as we diversify and expand services.

Services	Y1	Y2	Y3	Y4	Y5
Baby Coaching (1-hr visit)	100	150	225	338	506
Prenatal Classes ($199)	0	10	15	23	34
Prenatal Classes ($549)	0	8	12	18	27
Workshop (attendance)	0	0	100	150	225

Baby Coach pay per session	
Standard session	55
1-session class	92
3-session class	276

REFERENCES

1. Cawthorne, A., & Arons, J. (2010). *There's No Place Like Home*. Center for American Progress.
2. Center on the Developing Child at Harvard University. (2010). *The Foundations of Lifelong Health Are Built in Early Childhood*. https://www.developingchild.harvard.edu.
3. Daro, D., McCurdy, K., & Nelson, C. (2005, September). Engaging and Retaining Participants in Voluntary New Parent Support Programs. *Chapin Hall Center for Children at the University of Chicago Issue Brief* (104).
4. Every Child Matters Education Fund. (2010). *We Can Do Better: Child Abuse and Neglect Deaths in America*. Washington, DC: Every Child Matters Education Fund.
5. Fang, X., Brown, D., Florence, C., & Mercy, J. (2012). The economic burden of child maltreatment in the United States and implications for prevention. *Child Abuse & Neglect*, *36*: 156–165.
6. Gonzalez, A., & MacMillan, H. L. (2008). Preventing child maltreatment: An evidence-based update. *Journal of Postgraduate Medicine*. *54*(4): 280–286.
7. Healthy Families New York. (n.d.). *The Healthy Families New York (HFNY) Home Visiting Program: Findings from the Randomized Control Trial*.
8. Lee, S., Aos, S., Drake, E., Pennucci, A., Miller, M., & Anderson, L. (2012). *Return on Investment: Evidence-Based Options to Improve Statewide Outcomes, April 2012* (Document No. 12-04-1201). Olympia, WA: Washington State Institute for Public Policy.
9. Kamerman, S., & Kahn, A. (1993). Home health visiting in Europe. *The Future of Children*, *3*: 39–52.
10. The PEW Center on the States. (2010, May). The case for home visiting. *The PEW Home Visiting Campaign Issue Brief*.
11. U.S. Census Bureau. (2010). American Community Survey.
12. U.S. Department of Labor Bureau of Labor Statistics. (2012). *News Release: Employment Characteristics of Families 2011*. U.S. Department of Labor.

The Parent Universe Business Plan was authored by Patty Mojta, director of Parent Universe, which is a part of the nonprofit organization, Prevent Child Abuse New Jersey

---

GLOSSARY OF KEY TERMS AND CONCEPTS

You are likely to encounter some or all of the following terms and concepts as you pursue your career in social work management. Most, but not all, of these glossary items are explained in the chapters of this book. This glossary is designed to help orient you to new terminology, but is by no means exhaustive in its approach, and there may be other important items not included here.

Accounting—the language of business that is used to communicate financial information. Common accounting statements applicable to nonprofit organizations include the *balance sheet, income statement,* and *statement of cash flows.* The nonprofit accounting equation is Assets = Liabilities + Net Assets.

Acquisition—the process of one organization in effect taking over another by purchasing or somehow assuming its assets and liabilities. The organization making the acquisition is known as the *acquirer* and the organization being acquired is often called the *target.*

Annual report—a document produced by an organization containing program highlights for the year as well as financial information—typically a year-end balance sheet showing overall financial health. Annual reports can often be found on websites of organizations, often in the "about us" section.

208 GLOSSARY OF KEY TERMS AND CONCEPTS

Assets—anything an organization owns or claims, such as cash in the bank, accounts receivable, vehicles, property, etc. People are not owned by an organization and are, therefore, not assets in a technical accounting sense; however, the phrase *human assets* is sometimes used to refer to employees of an organization.

Balance sheet—illustrates the value of an organization's assets, liabilities, and net assets at a given point in time. Sometimes referred to as the *statement of financial position*, a balance sheet provides useful information on financial stability and health (e.g. the extent to which assets outweigh liabilities).

Budget—programs, projects, and organizations have budgets to plan and track revenue coming in and expenses going out. Staying on budget involves only spending what has been planned in the budget and, likewise, capturing revenue that has been planned. Deviation from the plan is referred to as *budget variance*.

Business plan—a tool for explaining a new program idea and the means by which it adds both social and financial value to an organization. Business planning in the social sector differs from traditional grant writing mainly because a business plan focuses on how the program idea will generate income to sustain it into the future.

Capital structure—a breakdown of how an organization or program is financed. Nonprofits, for example, usually contain a mix of grants, fee-for-service revenue, donations, debt, etc. as part of their capital structures. Government organizations often include tax revenue and debt (e.g. bonds sold to the public) in their capital structures.

Cash flows (statement of)—a table tracking the use of cash in an organization over a particular period of time. Cash flow statement categories include the movement of cash from operating, investing, and financing activities.

Compensation—a comprehensive term for describing how an employee is paid for work performed. Compensation ideally includes more than just salary. Benefits and other perks are also included in an employee's *total compensation*.

GLOSSARY OF KEY TERMS AND CONCEPTS   209

Communications—encompasses the functions of public relations, internal and external messaging, social media management, etc. An organization's communications processes are closely tied to its marketing and sales efforts.

Consultative selling—the process of building relationships with prospective customers, donors, clients, etc. to go beyond making a one-time sale or transaction. This type of selling builds long-term customer, donor, and client loyalty.

Diversification—a basic tenet of financial management. Essentially, the more numerous and varied an organization's portfolio of programs, for example, the less likely that the entire organization will fail if one of its programs encounters problems. Organizations should strive to build diversified portfolios of programs and revenue streams.

Earned income—unlike revenue from grants that is often given to an organization before any work takes place, earned income, such as fee-for-service revenue, must be made or earned during each transaction. A good example of earned income is money made by Girl Scouts for selling Girl Scout Cookies.

Effectiveness—whether a program or organization is actually achieving what is desired in a meaningful way. Achieving the mission of a program, for example, should mean that the particular program is effective.

Efficiency—using the least resources possible to carry out a mission. An efficient organization is not necessarily effective. Saving money and other resources may not produce the best results for an organization's clients. Efficiency and effectiveness are interrelated concepts.

Flextime—a practice in which employees are allowed to work flexible hours when possible. This can be an important benefit for employees as part of a total compensation package and is usually cost-neutral to the organization if managed properly.

Gross income—the total amount of revenue received by an organization or program (or in your paycheck) before any expenses are deducted.

210 GLOSSARY OF KEY TERMS AND CONCEPTS

Human resources—organizations have various types of resources: financial, technology, intellectual property, and also human resources, which are the people that produce the work of the organization.

Income statement—one of the key financial statements, the income statement is an illustration of the financial activity of an organization or program over a certain period of time. All income and expenses are recorded on this statement and the bottom line of the income statement denotes the *net income*—how much income is left after all expenses have been subtracted for the given time period.

Liabilities—anything that is owed by an organization (or what someone or something else owns or claims). This could include wages payable to employees, loans or lines of credit that must be repaid, pension commitments, etc.

Logic model—a diagram that explains how a program's activities produce outputs and outcomes from the program's inputs. The logic model visually presents how a client, in theory, enters a program, participates, and exits the program having achieved certain outputs and outcomes.

Margin—another word for profit, margin is essentially the amount of money that is retained by an organization after all expenses have been paid. Margin (and profit) is often expressed as a percentage (e.g. a program operating at a 5 percent margin means that 5 percent of the money that went into the program is left over after all program expenses have been met).

Marketing—all of the activities involved in preparing a product or service for successful sales in the marketplace. Marketing involves activities such as segmenting, targeting, and positioning in the marketplace, as well as pricing, distribution, promotion and advertising, etc.

Merger—the joining of two organizations. Mergers are becoming more common in nonprofit and government sectors as budgetary and other pressures make it necessary for organizations to conserve resources and sustain impact by joining together.

GLOSSARY OF KEY TERMS AND CONCEPTS   211

Metric—another word for measurement. The term metric is used often in the for-profit sector. Metrics can be benchmarks or milestones that are set by organizations or by funders. These benchmarks are used to measure performance.

Monetization—the process of translating social outcomes into financial, specifically monetary, language. For example, an organization might claim, in an effort to garner donations for its efforts, that it costs $22,000 to feed a homeless family of four for a year. Donors can more easily "shop around" to see which organizations offer the best value when outcomes are monetized.

Net assets—part of the basic accounting equation, net assets represent the value of assets left over after all liabilities have been covered. Organizations with higher net assets are typically in better financial health.

Net income (surplus, profit)—from the income statement, net income, often referred to as the *bottom line* or *profit*, is the amount of income that is left after all expenses have been paid during a certain period of time. Net income is often referred to as *surplus* in the nonprofit sector.

Organizational chart—a diagram showing the structure of an organization or program. This chart can quickly explain who reports to whom and where various people reside within an organization.

Outcomes—the ultimate goals of a program or organization, outcomes are often stated or implied in mission statements. In a job-training program, for example, one desired outcome might be that a participant obtains and maintains a new job for a period of one year.

Outputs—immediate results stemming from the activities of a program or organization. In a job-training program, for example, an output might be that a participant fills out a job application. Outputs are not as impactful as outcomes.

Profit—see *net income.*

Pro forma—in business settings, pro forma financial statements are prepared and estimated in advance of a planned transaction. Pro forma financial statements are used in business plan documents to estimate the performance of a new business idea into the future. Importantly, pro forma financial statements are estimates and may not actually represent future performance.

Return on investment (ROI)—a commonly used term in the financial industry, ROI is the amount (or percentage) of money an investor can expect to receive in return after making an investment. In the social sector, *social return on investment (SROI)* is a more commonly used term—see below.

Sales—the process of convincing a customer that he or she should purchase a product or service. Successful sales efforts are based on a solid marketing foundation.

Social entrepreneurship—innovative ideas for social change executed utilizing sound business management strategies and skills. Social entrepreneurship is effectively the merging of social work management practice with business acumen. Depending on the context, social entrepreneurship can be described as social enterprise, social innovation, social purpose business venturing, etc.

Social impact—in a social entrepreneurship framework, social impact represents the magnitude of change that a particular program or organization makes with an individual, family, or community. A complementary concept is financial sustainability—the extent to which a particular program or organization can generate enough revenue to continue its operations.

Social return on investment (SROI)—built on the concept of *return on investment (ROI)*, SROI is the idea that an investor seeks a non-monetary return on a financial investment. The concept is still somewhat nebulous and is debated, but nonetheless, SROI is an important concept with which to be familiar because certain investors (e.g. donors, foundations, etc.) want to measure the amount of social good that their investments create.

GLOSSARY OF KEY TERMS AND CONCEPTS 213

Stretch assignment—a work task that is outside of one's normal responsibilities and taken on out of a desire to enhance one's knowledge base and position oneself for career advancement.

Surplus—see *net income.*

Talent—a new way of referring to an organization's human resources. In many service industries, including the human services, the level of combined talent and expertise of an organization's team determines the effectiveness of services.

Total compensation—see *compensation.*

Unrelated business income (UBI)—in the nonprofit sector, revenue that is generated by activities not related to an organization's mission. For example, a family services agency that sells Christmas trees in its parking lot for the sole purpose of making money for the organization is participating in unrelated business. UBI is allowed up to a certain limit, but can have tax implications.

Venture philanthropy—based on the practice of venture capital investing in which investors make strategic investments in growing companies and also work closely with management teams, venture philanthropists seek to make investments in social-sector organizations to create significant impact. Here, the focus is mainly on SROI, although some venture philanthropists may also seek financial returns.

REFERENCES

Anderson, B. B., Dees, J. G., & Emerson, J. (2002). Developing viable earned income strategies. In J. G. Dees, J. Emerson, & P. Economy (Eds.), *Strategic tools for social entrepreneurs: Enhancing the performance of your enterprising nonprofit* (pp. 191–233). New York: John Wiley & Sons.

Andreasen, A. R., & Kotler, P. (2003). *Strategic marketing for nonprofit organizations*, 6th edition. Upper Saddle River, NJ: Prentice Hall.

Ayers, G. W., Mindel, C. H., Robinson, L., & Wright, J. (1981). Fees in a human service agency: Why do clients pay? *Social Work*, *26*(3): 245–248.

Banjo, S. (2010, June 9). *Donations slip amid anxiety.* Retrieved November 3, 2011, from the *Wall Street Journal* website: http://online.wsj.com/article/SB1000142405274 8704256604575294913333857770.html.

Bell, J., Moyers, R., & Wolfred, T. (2006). *Daring to lead 2006: A national study of nonprofit executive leadership.* Oakland, CA: CompassPoint Nonprofit Services/ Washington, DC: Meyer Foundation.

Bornstein, D. (2004). *How to change the world: Social entrepreneurs and the power of new ideas.* New York: Oxford University Press.

Brewster, R. (2006). *Social enterprise: Introducing earned income ventures into your nonprofit organization.* Lecture at Baruch College's School of Public Affairs, October 12, 2006.

Brinckerhoff, P. C. (2000). *Social entrepreneurship: The art of mission-based venture development.* New York: John Wiley & Sons.

Brody, R. (2005). *Effectively managing human service organizations*, 3rd edition. Thousand Oaks, CA: Sage.

Brooks, A. C. (2009). *Social entrepreneurship: A modern approach to social value creation.* Upper Saddle River, NJ: Pearson Prentice Hall.

Brothers, J., & Sherman, A. (2012). *Building nonprofit capacity: A guide to managing change through organizational lifecycles.* San Francisco, CA: Jossey-Bass.

Brown, W. A. (2010). Strategic management. In D. Renz (Ed.), *The Jossey-Bass handbook of nonprofit leadership and management* (pp. 206–229). San Francisco, CA: Jossey-Bass.

Carman, J. G. (2009). Nonprofits, funders, and evaluation: Accountability in action. *American Review of Public Administration, 39*(4): 374–390.

Carman, J. G. (2011). Understanding evaluation in nonprofit organizations. *Public Performance & Management Review, 34*(3): 350–377.

The Center for Nonprofits. (2013). *NJ non-profit survey: Some hopeful signs tempered by rising demand, funding uncertainties.* Retrieved March 28, 2013, from The Center for Nonprofits website: www.njnonprofits.org/PressRelease2013NonprofitSurvey.pdf.

Chicago Sun-Times. (2010, November 29). Charitable giving up; demand higher. Retrieved November 3, 2011, from the *Chicago Sun-Times* website: www.suntimes.com/news/nation/2606661-418/charitable-giving-donations-nonprofit-reported.html.

Cohen, R. (2012, August 2). *Death of the Hull House: A nonprofit coroner's request.* Retrieved September 2, 2012, from the Nonprofit Quarterly website: www.nonprofitquarterly.org/management/20758-death-of-the-hullhouse-a-nonprofit-coroners-inquest.html.

Conaty, B., & Charan, R. (2010). *The talent masters: Why smart leaders put people before numbers.* New York: Crown Business.

Dart, R. (2004). The legitimacy of social enterprise. *Nonprofit Leadership & Management, 14*(4), 411–424.

Donovan, D. (2013, January 1). *Fiscal cliff deal could hurt charitable giving.* Retrieved January 1, 2013, from the Chronicle of Philanthropy website: http://philanthropy.com/blogs/government-and-politics/fiscal-cliff-deal-could-hurt-charitable-giving/31559.

The Economist. (2012, January 28). *Grabbing Grameen: Property rights in peril in Bangladesh.* Retrieved August 15, 2013, from *The Economist* website: www.economist.com/node/21543547.

Egan, M., & Kadushin, G. (1999). The social worker in the emerging field of home care: Professional activities and ethical concerns. *Health & Social Work, 24*(1): 43–55.

Firstenberg, P. B. (1986). *Managing for profit in the nonprofit world.* New York: The Foundation Center.

Fleischer, A. (2013, January 4). The taxman's uncharitable new rule [Editorial]. *The Wall Street Journal*, p. A11.

Forbes Funds. (2004). *Look here! Attracting and developing the next generation of nonprofit leaders.* Retrieved June 10, 2012, from the Forbes Funds website: www.forbesfunds.org.

Frazier, E. (2011). *Nonprofit hiring shows signs of recovery in 2011, new survey of employers finds.* Retrieved July 15, 2013, from the Chronicle of Philanthropy website: http://philanthropy.com/article/Outlook-for-Nonprofit-Staffing/127134.

Froelich, K. A. (1999). Diversification of revenue strategies: Evolving resource dependence in nonprofit organizations. In J. S. Ott (Ed.), *Understanding nonprofit organizations: Governance, leadership, and management* (pp. 182–194). Boulder, CO: Westview Press.

Furman, R., & Gibelman, M. (2013). *Navigating human service organizations: Essential information for thriving and surviving in agencies.* Chicago, IL: Lyceum Books.

Germak, A. J. (2013). Guest editorial note, *Administration in Social Work, 37*(2): 103–105.

Germak, A. J. (2013, March 4). ObamaCare's mandate and employment consequences [Letter to the editor]. *The Wall Street Journal*, p. A14.

Germak, A. J. (2013, April 27). Obama budget "taxes" charities by limiting deductions [Editorial]. *The Star-Ledger*, p. 4.

Germak, A. J. (2013, May 8). Ignoring addiction is ignoring dignity [Letter to the editor]. *Financial Times*, p. 6.

Germak, A. J. (2013, June 27). Time is ripe for social workers from China and U.S. to collaborate [Editorial]. *Global Times*, p. 15.

Germak, A. J. (2012, March 11). Tinkering with tax incentives could shift how rich share wealth [Editorial]. *The Star-Ledger*, p. 5 (section 2).

Germak, A. J., & Singh, K. K. (2010). Social entrepreneurship: Changing the way social workers do business. *Administration in Social Work, 34*(1): 79–95.

Giffords, E. D. (2000). A study of employee commitment in public, not-for-profit and proprietary social service organizations. *Dissertation Abstracts International, 61*(3): AAT9965250.

Gill, S. J. (2010). *Developing a learning culture in nonprofit organizations.* Thousand Oaks, CA: Sage.

Gummer, B. (1997). Is the code of ethics as applicable to agency executives as it is to direct service providers? No. In E. Gambrill & R. Pruger (Eds.), *Controversial issues in social work ethics, values, and obligations* (pp. 143–150). Boston, MA: Allyn & Bacon.

Guo, B. (2006). The marketization of human service nonprofits: Charity at risk? *Dissertation Abstracts International, 66*(10): AAT3191288.

Harding, R. (2004). Social enterprise: The new economic engine. *Business Strategy Review, 15*(4), 39–43.

Herman, R. D., & Renz, D. O. (2008). Advancing nonprofit organizational effectiveness research and theory: Nine theses. *Nonprofit Management & Leadership*, 18(4): 399–415.

Hopkins, B. R. (2009). *The law of tax-exempt organizations,* 9th edition. Hoboken, NJ: Wiley.

Horngren, C. T., Sundem, G. L., & Elliott, J. A. (2002). *Introduction to financial accounting.* Upper Saddle River, NJ: Pearson.

Independent Sector. (2013). *Scope of the nonprofit sector.* Retrieved July 31, 2013, from the Independent Sector website: www.independentsector.org/scope_of_the_ sector.

Kadushin, A., & Harkness, D. (2002). *Supervision in social work,* 4th edition. New York: Columbia University Press.

REFERENCES

Kerlin, J. A. (2010). A comparative analysis of the global emergence of social enterprise. *Voluntas: International Journal of Voluntary and Nonprofit Organizations, 21*(2): 162–179.

Kettner, P. M. (2002). *Achieving excellence in the management of human service organizations.* Boston, MA: Allyn & Bacon.

Kettner, P. M., Moroney, R. M., & Martin, L. L. (2008). *Designing and managing programs: An effectiveness-based approach,* 3rd edition. Thousand Oaks, CA: Sage.

Kickul, J., & Lyons, T. S. (2012). *Understanding social entrepreneurship: The relentless pursuit of mission in an ever changing world.* New York: Routledge.

Kurzman, P. A. (1976). Private practice as a social work function. *Social Work, 21*(5): 363–369.

Kurzman, P. A. (2000). Bakalinsky's conundrum: Should social workers practice in the world of work? *Administration in Social Work, 23*(3/4): 157–161.

Levinson, J. C. (1998). *Guerrilla marketing: Secrets for making big profits from your small business,* 3rd edition. New York: Houghton Mifflin Company.

Lewis, J. A., Packard, T. R., & Lewis, M. D. (2012). *Management of human service programs,* 5th edition. Belmont, CA: Brooks/Cole.

Light, P. C. (2006). Reshaping social entrepreneurship. *Stanford Social Innovation Review, 4*(3), 47–51.

Linn, A. (2013, June 22). *Charitable giving continues to be a victim of recession.* Retrieved June 23, 2013, from the CNBC website: www.cnbc.com/id/100829583.

Lynch-Cerullo, K., & Cooney, K. (2011). Moving from outputs to outcomes: A review of the evolution of performance measurement in the human service nonprofit sector. *Administration in Social Work, 35*(4): 364–388.

Martin, L. L., & Kettner, P. M. (1997). Performance measurement: The new accountability. *Administration in Social Work, 21*(1): 17–29.

Masi, D. A. (1992). Should social workers work for for-profit firms? Yes. In E. Gambrill & R. Pruger (Eds.), *Controversial issues in social work* (pp. 28–30). Boston, MA: Allyn & Bacon.

Maas, K. E., & Liket, K. C. (2011). Do we know what we are talking about? Measurement validity in social impact research. *Paper Presentation at Association for Research on Nonprofit Organizations and Voluntary Action Annual Conference,* November 19, Toronto, Canada.

Mathis, R. L., & Jackson, J. H. (2011). *Human resource management,* 13th edition. Mason, OH: South-Western Cengage Learning.

Messmer, M., & Bogardus, A. (2008). *Human resource management.* Hoboken, NJ: Wiley.

Mosher-Williams, R. (Ed.) (2006). *Research on social entrepreneurship: Understanding and contributing to an emerging field.* Retrieved June 1, 2006, from the ARNOVA website: www.arnova.org/publications.php.

Murray, V. (2010). Evaluating the effectiveness of nonprofit organizations. In D. Renz (Ed.), *The Jossey-Bass handbook of nonprofit leadership and management* (pp. 431–458). San Francisco, CA: Jossey-Bass.

REFERENCES

National Association of Social Workers (NASW) (1998). *Current controversies in social work ethics: Case examples.* Washington, DC: NASW Press.

National Association of Social Workers (NASW) (1999). *NASW's code of ethics.* Retrieved October 25, 2006, from www.ncsss.cua.edu/Docs/NASWCodeofEthics.pdf.

Nayar, V. (2010). *Employees first, customers second: Turning conventional management upside down.* Boston, MA: Harvard Business Press.

Nonprofit Finance Fund. (2013). *Nonprofit finance fund survey of 5900+ nonprofits: Organizations innovating and adapting to new reality.* Retrieved March 26, 2013, from the Nonprofit Finance Fund website: http://nonprofitfinancefund.org/announcements/2013/state-of-the-nonprofit-sector-survey.

Norwegian Nobel Committee. (2006). *Norwegian Nobel Committee's 2006 Nobel Peace Prize Announcement (2006).* Retrieved October 22, 2006, from the Nobel Prize website: www.nobelprize.org/nobel_prizes/peace/laureates/2006/press.html.

Oster, S. (1995). *Strategic management for nonprofit organizations.* New York: Oxford University Press.

Pallotta, D. (2008). *Uncharitable: How restraints on nonprofits undermine their potential.* Medford, MA: Tufts University Press.

Pallotta, D. (2012). *Charity case: How the nonprofit community can stand up for itself and really change the world.* San Francisco, CA: Jossey-Bass.

Patti, R. (2009). Management in human services: Purposes, practice, and prospects in the 21st century. In R. Patti (Ed.), *The Handbook of Human Services Management*, 2nd edition (pp. 3–28). Thousand Oaks, CA: Sage.

Porter, M. E. (1980). *Competitive strategy: Techniques for analyzing industries and competitors.* New York: The Free Press.

Porter, M. E. (1985). *Competitive advantage: Creating and sustaining superior performance.* New York: The Free Press.

Ridley-Duff, R., & Bull, M. (2011). *Understanding social enterprise: Theory and practice.* Thousand Oaks, CA: Sage.

Ritchie, W. J., & Kolodinsky, R. W. (2003). Nonprofit organization financial performance measurement: An evaluation of new and existing financial performance measures. *Nonprofit Management & Leadership*, *13*(4): 367.

Roberts, D., & Woods, C. (2005). Changing the world on a shoestring: The concept of social entrepreneurship. *University of Auckland Business Review*, *7*(1), 45–51.

Salamon, L. M. (1999). *America's nonprofit sector: A primer.* New York: The Foundation Center.

Samuelson, W. F., & Marks, S. G. (2003). *Managerial economics.* New York: John Wiley & Sons.

Sandfort, J. R. (2010). Human service organizational technology: Improving understanding and advancing research. In Y. Hasenfeld (Ed.), *Human services as complex organizations* (pp. 269–290). Thousand Oaks, CA: Sage.

Schiller, R. J. (2012, December 16). Please don't mess with the charitable deduction [Editorial]. *The New York Times*, p. BU7.

Score Foundation. (2010). *Business planning tools for nonprofit organizations*, 2nd edition. Retrieved May 15, 2013, from the Score Foundation website: www.score.org/sites/default/files/BizPlanningforNonProfits_0.pdf.

Solomon, J., & Sandahl, Y. (2007). *Stepping up or stepping out: A report on the readiness of next generation leaders*. Retrieved June 25, 2012, from the Young Nonprofit Professionals Network website: http://ynpn.org/wp-content/uploads/stepping_up.pdf.

Tekula, R. (2010). Social enterprise: Innovation or mission distraction. Working Paper, Pace University, Wilson Center for Social Entrepreneurship. Retrieved October 12, 2011, from the Pace University website: www.pace.edu/emplibrary/TEKULA_Social%20Enterprise_Innovation%20or%20Mission%20Distraction.pdf.

Thomson, D. E. (2011). The role of funders in driving nonprofit performance measurement and use in strategic management. *Public Performance & Management Review, 35*(1): 54–78.

Tierney, T. J. (2006). The leadership deficit. *Stanford Social Innovation Review, 4*(2): 26–35.

Tropman, J. E. (2006). Producing high-quality group decisions. In R. L. Edwards & J. A. Yankey (Eds.), *Effectively managing nonprofit organizations* (pp. 215–238). Washington, DC: NASW Press.

Wang, X. (2002). Perception and reality in developing an outcome performance measurement system. *International Journal of Public Administration, 25*(6): 805–829.

Watkins, M. (2003). *The first 90 days: Critical success strategies for new leaders at all levels*. Boston, MA: Harvard Business School Press.

Wei-Skillern, J., Austin, J. E., Leonard, H., & Stevenson, H. (2007). *Entrepreneurship in the social sector*. Thousand Oaks, CA: Sage.

Weinbach, R. W., & Taylor, L. M. (2011). *The social worker as manager: A practical guide to success*, 6th edition. Boston, MA: Allyn & Bacon.

Weisbrod, B. A. (1998). Commercialism and the road ahead. In J. S. Ott (Ed.), *Understanding nonprofit organizations: Governance, leadership, and management* (pp. 231–238). Boulder, CO: Westview Press.

Wimpfheimer, S., & Germak, A. J. (2012, March). *Social work managers as entrepreneurs: Skills for the new economy*. Workshop presentation at the annual symposium of the National Association of Social Workers (NASW)—Massachusetts Chapter, Framingham, MA.

Zietlow, J., Hankin, J. A., & Seidner, A. (2007). *Financial management for nonprofit organizations: Policies and practices*. Hoboken, NJ: Wiley.

INDEX

accounting 28–32; financial statements 32–38
Anderson, B.B. 9–10
annualizing 39–41
appendices 114–116
Apps 151
ARNOVA 121
assets 30–32, 129
Ayers, G.W. 146

balance sheet 32–33
Bangladesh 10–11
board of directors 64, 67–71, 91
Bornstein, D. 10
Brewster, R. 8–9
Brody, R. 62
Brooks, A.C. 126
Brothers, J. 64
Brown, W.A. 131
budgets 28–29
Bull, M. 130
business climate 140–143
business plan 103–104, 116–117; components of 107–116; internet resources 118–119; learning exercises 117–118; reasons for 104–107

business, service 52–55
business skills 1–2, 4–5, 18–20, 160; key points 155–159; meetings 95 *see also* social entrepreneurship

capital structure 43–44
cash flows 36–38
charitable tax deduction 140–141
commercial activity 10
communication 79–80, 92–98; internet resources 100–101; learning exercises 99–100 *see also* e-mail
community 57
compensation 62–63, 141–143
competition 8, 110–111
connections 72–73
customer/client 52–54; feedback 54–55

Dart, R. 8
Dees, J.G. 9–10
development 61–62, 64
downward management 55–63

e-mail 95–97, 147–148
economic theory 10
effectiveness *see* performance measurement

Egan, M. 145
elevator pitch 93–94
emerging issues: internet resources 153–154; learning exercises 152–153
emerging technology 146–151
Emerson, J. 9–10
entrepreneurship *see* social entrepreneurship
ethics 143–146; and technology 146–151
evaluation *see* program evaluation
executive summary 108–109
expenses 35, 38–43
external selling 89–92

feedback 54–55
financial health 26–28, 32
financial management 25–28, 38–39, 45; internet resources 46–47; learning exercises 46; and talent management 50–52
financial plan 112–113
financial statements 32–38, 41–43
financial sustainability *see* sustainability
firm performance *see* performance
for-profit organizations 16–17, 26, 129–130
forecasting *see* projecting
Four P's framework 80–83, 112
Froelich, K.A. 9–10, 145
functional expenses 35
funding 12, 44, 79, 91, 104; and outputs/outcomes 126–127
Furman, R. 85

Gibelman, M. 85
Gill, S.J. 126
Grameen Bank 10–11
grants *see* funding
Gummer, B. 144

Hankin, J.A. 31–32
Harkness, D. 62
health insurance 50–52, 142–143
hiring 57–58

human service organizations 5–7, 49–50; measurement and 130–131; and talent 55–56; technology and 146–151
hybrid organizations 17

impact 121–124, 128, 131, 133–137
income statement 33–35, 41–43
internal selling 87–89
Internet resources 21–23; business plan 118–119; emerging issues 153–154; financial management 46–47; marketing/sales/communication 100–101; performance measurement 137–138; talent management 75–77
internships 56–57

Jackson, J.H. 61
jobs *see* hiring

Kadushin, A. 62
Kadushin, G. 145
Kickul, J. 125
Knight, W. 133–136
Kurzman, P.A. 145–146

learning exercises 20–21; business plan 117–118; emerging issues 152–153; financial management 46; marketing/sales/communication 99–100; performance measurement 137; talent management 74–75
Levinson, J.C. 86
liabilities 30–32
Light, P. 9
LinkedIn 73, 149
Loch, C. 67–71, 91
logic models 132–133
Lyons, T.S. 125

management *see* financial management; social work managers; talent management
management team 113–114
marketing 79–80, 98; analysis 109–111; frameworks 80–84, 111–112; internet

resources 100–101; learning exercises 99–100; plan 85–87, 111–112; research 85

Masi, D.A. 144

Mathis, R.L. 61

measurement 125–137

media 91–92

meetings 95–96

Mindel, C.H. 146

mobile devices 150–151

modeling 41–43 *see also* logic models

Mojta, P. 116

money 14

Mosher-Williams, R. 8

motivation 88–89

MTI Business Development, Inc. 133–136

Murray, V. 131

National Association of Social Workers 143–146

Nayar, V. 53

net assets 30–32

networks 72–73

New York Times 7

no money, no mission 26–27

nonprofit organizations 14–16, 26, 126; accounting 28–38; business climate 140–143; capital structure 43–44; role of board 64, 67–71

Obama, B. 140

operations plan 112

organizations 5–7, 14–18; measuring effectiveness 125–131; workforce structure 58–61

Oster, S. 131

outputs/outcomes 126–128

Pallota, D. 122, 130, 142

Parent Universe 116

Patient Protection and Affordable Care Act 142–143

performance appraisal 61, 97–98

performance management 61–62

performance measurement 121–131; internet resources 137–138; learning exercises 137

personnel 113–114 *see also* talent management

philanthropy 7

pitch 3–5, 93–95

Porter, M.E. 110

presentations 3

pro forma statements 41–43

profit organizations 16–17, 26, 129–130

program concept 109

program evaluation 124–131

projecting 38–41

Prototypes, Inc 67–71

research 85, 110

revenue 38–43

Ridley-Duff, R. 130

Robinson, L. 146

sales 79–80, 87–92, 98; internet resources 100–101; learning exercises 99–100

sales pitch 3–5, 94–95

Sandfort, J.R. 127

Seidner, A. 31–32

selling *see* sales

service business 52–55

Sherman, A. 64

sideways management 71–73

social entrepreneurship 7–11; ethical considerations 143–146; example of 11–14

social impact *see* impact

social media/networks 73, 148–150

social work 1–2; internships 56–57; measurement and 130–131; as a service business 52–55; and technology 146–151

social work managers 2–5; employment 14–18; environment of 5–7, 11–14, 139–143; ethical considerations 143–146; finance and 25–28, 38–39

stakeholders 92, 126–127
statement of cash flows 36–38
statement of functional expenses 35
STP framework 82–84, 111
strategic networks 72
stretch assignments 66
structuring, of organizations 58–61
succession planning 65
supervisor relations 65–66
supply and demand 10
sustainability 121–124, 128, 130–131, 133–137, 146

talent management 49–50, 55–56, 73–74; development 61–62; downward 55–63; and financial management 50–52; internet resources 75–77; learning exercises 74–75; sideways 71–73; upward 63–71
talent pipeline 56–57

tax deduction 140–141
Taylor, L.M. 61
technology 146–151
total compensation 62–63
training 62
transactions 55–56
Tropman, J.E. 95
two-minute pitch 4

upward management 63–71
U.S. economy 104, 140–143

Watkins, M. 72
Weinbach, R.W. 61
Weisbrod, B.A. 10
workforce 58–61
Wright, J. 146

Yunus, M. 10–11

Zietlow, J. 31–32